To the
Glory of God

*A 40-Day Devotional
on the Book of Romans*

James Montgomery Boice
Compiled by D. Marion Clark

BakerBooks

a division of Baker Publishing Group
Grand Rapids, Michigan

© 2010 by Linda M. Boice

Published by Baker Books
a division of Baker Publishing Group
P.O. Box 6287, Grand Rapids, MI 49516-6287
www.bakerbooks.com

Printed in the United States of America

Library of Congress Cataloging-in-Publication Data
Boice, James Montgomery, 1938–2000.
  To the glory of God : a 40-day devotional on the book of Romans / James Montgomery Boice ; compiled by D. Marion Clark.
     p.   cm.
  Includes bibliographical references.
  ISBN 978-0-8010-7279-6 (pbk.)
    1. Bible. N.T. Romans—Meditations. I. Clark, Marion (D. Marion). II. Title.
BS2665.54.B65 2010
242′.5—dc22   2009054421

Scripture is taken from the HOLY BIBLE, NEW INTERNATIONAL VERSION®. NIV®. Copyright © 1973, 1978, 1984 by International Bible Society. Used by permission of Zondervan. All rights reserved.

10   11   12   13   14   15   16   7   6   5   4   3   2   1

Contents

Foreword

Reading the book of Romans will change your life.

This was the experience of the early Christians in Rome, who first received Romans as an epistle from the apostle Paul. It was also the experience of Augustine, the North African theologian who heard God's call to a life of gospel holiness while he was reading Romans 13 in a private garden. Romans changed Martin Luther's life too. One of the crucial theological breakthroughs that brought reformation to Germany was Luther's discovery that the righteousness of God in Romans 1 was a gift, not a threat.

Over the centuries, many other men and women have testified that Paul's letter to the Romans helped them understand the gift of God's saving grace and offer their lives in service to God. This was certainly the testimony of Dr. James Montgomery Boice, the outstanding preacher whose wise comments on Romans provide the content for the forty entries in this book of daily devotions.

Dr. Boice served for more than thirty years as the senior minister of Philadelphia's Tenth Presbyterian Church. Over the years he preached long series of sermons through many books of the Bible. Yet none of them had a greater impact than the eight years he spent carefully working his way through Romans, week by week and verse by verse. The four-volume commentary that came out of those sermons is part of Dr. Boice's lasting legacy for the church. Now the essence of his teaching through Romans is summarized in the form of daily devotions.

The foundation for this book is the text of Romans itself, which is printed in its entirety. The text is organized according to Dr. Boice's broad outline of Romans, enabling readers to trace the logic of the apostle Paul: Justification by Faith (chapters 1–4); The Reign of Grace (chapters 5–8); God and History (chapters 9–11); and The New Humanity (chapters 12–16).

Dr. Boice's friend and colleague Marion Clark has carefully and skillfully selected these devotions to cover the most important texts in Romans, including many of Dr. Boice's particular favorites. All of the great doctrines of salvation are here: the wages of original sin, the justifying righteousness of Jesus Christ, the gracious gift of saving faith, the sovereign election of God, and the mind-renewing work of the Holy Spirit.

As you will discover, Dr. Boice had a rare gift for clarity in communicating the Word of God. In these devotions he makes the gospel clear for people who have not yet committed their lives to Jesus Christ. He also makes the implications of Christian theology clear for people who have decided to follow Jesus. It is not just the doctrines of Romans that Dr. Boice makes clear, but also their practical implications for everyday discipleship. Pastor Clark has taken the application of biblical truth one step farther by ending each devotional with a searching question or a word of wise spiritual counsel.

My prayer is that God will continue to bless Dr. Boice's teaching ministry as you read these devotions, as the Holy Spirit gives you the life-changing experience of understanding, believing, and applying the book of Romans.

Philip Graham Ryken
President, Wheaton College

Preface

It has been in the back of my mind for a while to put together a yearlong devotional book from the writings of James Montgomery Boice. I served under Dr. Boice for eleven years, first as principal of the college preparatory school he founded with his wife, Linda, and then as executive minister of Tenth Presbyterian Church. I learned many valuable lessons and skills from Dr. Boice, but none more important than the sufficiency of Scripture. In a time in which I was seeking more "meaningful" experiences, he led me by example and teaching to value the great experience of having God's revealed Word in my hands. Dr. Boice preached Scripture; he did not dip into Scripture. He preached it out of conviction that God's Word alone is sufficient to reveal to us what we need to make us "wise for salvation" and to be "thoroughly equipped for every good work" (2 Tim. 3:15, 17).

As the tenth anniversary of Dr. Boice's death (June 15, 2000) drew closer and I was thinking of an appropriate way to honor his ministry, the idea of the devotional returned. This time I decided to provide a shorter devotional that the members of Tenth Presbyterian Church could read as we observe this anniversary together. It seemed most natural to turn to Dr. Boice's commentary on Romans, the book he spent eight years preaching on at the church.

These devotions are mostly drawn from the conclusions of his sermons, in which Dr. Boice drove home the lessons of the Scripture passage under study. My prayer is that readers will be moved by the insights he astutely presents and by the way he presses them home on the mind and heart.

As one can imagine, the paring-down process was challenging. Culling forty selections from 239 sermons was a formidable task. Even more heart-wrenching was editing each piece to fit the word limitations. Two features of Dr. Boice's preaching led me to skip over many sermon conclusions or to spend extra time paring down the conclusions. One is that he often quoted other writers extensively, even unabashedly using their outlines for a message. Dr. Boice openly appreciated the writings of other commentators and preachers. Indeed, he freely quoted from them in hopes that his listeners would read their books. Second, he used other Scripture passages as commentary. In many cases, his conclusions would have made it appear that I had borrowed from a commentary on a different book of the Bible altogether.

You will quickly discover how evangelistic Dr. Boice's preaching was, especially in regard to the passages covering the first four chapters of Romans. I had envisioned this devotional primarily as a book to encourage the faithful in their Christian walk. Yet most of the first half of the devotional is taken up in direct appeals to receive the gospel. Without knowing the background of these sermons, one might think they were preached at an evangelistic crusade. They certainly reveal Dr. Boice's heart for the lost. As respected as he was for his erudition, his preaching was practical, with the intent to see hearts changed through the teaching of God's Word. That certainly was Dr. Boice's desire for the Romans messages. As he says in his own preface to the first of four volumes:

> We all fear change, of course. It makes us anxious. But change is precisely what we need. If we are spiritually moribund, we need to be brought from a state of spiritual death into a

state of spiritual life through the gospel. If we are lethargic in our discipleship, we need to be awakened to the glories of a renewed life in Christ. If we are indifferent to the spiritual state of others, we need to be alerted to their peril apart from Christ and be moved to take the gospel to them.[1]

I want to thank Phil Ryken for his encouragement to start this project and for his ongoing advice throughout the process. Linda Boice reviewed the manuscript and was especially helpful in editing the comments added to the end of each devotion. My wife, Ginger, also reviewed the manuscript, and her insights led to tighter alignment between each devotion and its Scripture text. Thanks also go to Baker Books, specifically Bob Hosack, who led the process from acceptance of the manuscript to its final form. I approached Baker because it published most of Dr. Boice's commentaries. I hope this devotional will leave readers desiring to read the treasure of commentaries and other books Dr. Boice left us. I should also note the invaluable aid of having the Boice Expositional Commentaries on CD-ROM.

My desire for these devotions is expressed by Dr. Boice's concluding words in the preface to his final volume on Romans:

It was Paul's deepest desire that everything he did and every thought he had might be to the glory of the great, sovereign, wise, holy, and compassionate God who had saved him through the gospel of his Son, Jesus Christ.

That is my desire too. And it is my special desire for this specific attempt to teach Romans. May God bless it to many people now and for many years to come. May it help them come to know him better and obey him. To God alone be the glory.[2]

D. Marion Clark
Tenth Presbyterian Church
Philadelphia, Pennsylvania

Introduction

In any other circumstances and by any other hand, the letter written to the church in Rome might have been a mere incidental piece of correspondence. But the author of this letter was the apostle Paul, and by his hand and under the guidance of the Holy Spirit, this bit of ancient writing became for Christians one of the most influential documents ever penned.

In the fourth century a distinguished philosopher and teacher named Augustine was under conviction concerning the truthfulness of Christianity. He was a brilliant man, but he had lived an immoral life, as many of the pagan intellectuals of his day did, and his past practice of immorality held him in a vise-like grip. He tells about his immoral life in the eighth book of his *Confessions*, relating how, although he was convinced of the truthfulness of Christianity, he nevertheless kept putting off a true repudiation of sin and a commitment to Jesus Christ.

One day, while in the garden of a friend's estate near Milan, Italy, Augustine heard a child singing the words *tole lege, tole lege* ("take and read"). He had never heard the song before, so he received it as a message from God. Obeying the message, he rushed to a Bible, opened it at random, and began to read the words that first met his astonished gaze. They were from Romans 13: "Let us behave decently, as in the daytime, not in orgies and drunkenness, not in sexual immorality and debauchery, not in dissension and jealousy. Rather, clothe yourselves with the Lord Jesus Christ, and do not think about how to gratify the desires of the sinful nature" (vv. 13–14). This was exactly what St. Augustine, as he was later called, needed to read. The words were the means of his conversion. Afterward he wrote, "Instantly, as the sentence ended—by a light, as it were, of security infused into my heart—all the gloom of doubt was vanished away."[1] Augustine became the greatest figure in the early Christian church between the apostle Paul and Martin Luther.

A second example of the epistle's influence concerns the Protestant Reformer Martin Luther. He was no profligate, as Augustine was. Quite the contrary. Luther was a pious, earnest monk—an apparent Christian. But Luther had no peace of soul. He wanted to please God, to be accepted by him. But the harder he worked, the more elusive the salvation of his soul seemed to be. Instead of growing closer to God, he found himself moving away from him. Instead of loving God, which Luther knew he should do, he found himself hating God for requiring an apparently impossible standard of righteousness for human beings.

In desperation Luther turned to a study of Paul's letter to the Romans, and there, as early as the seventeenth verse of chapter 1, he found the solution: "For in the gospel a righteousness from God is revealed, a righteousness that is by faith from first to last, just as it is written: 'The righteous will live by faith.'" As God opened the meaning of this verse to him, Luther realized that the righteousness he needed was not his own righteousness but a righteousness of God, freely given to all who would receive it. Furthermore, this righteousness was to be received not through any works of his own but by faith only (*sola fide*). Faith meant taking God at his word, believing him. Luther did this, and as he did, he felt reborn and as if he had entered Paradise. Here is how he put it:

I had no love for that holy and just God who punishes sinners. I was filled with secret anger against him. I hated him, because, not content with frightening by the law and the miseries of life us wretched sinners, already ruined by original sin, he still further increased our tortures by the gospel. . . . But when, by the Spirit of God, I understood the words— when I learned how the justification of the sinner proceeds from the free mercy of our Lord through faith . . . then I felt born again like a new man. . . . In very truth, this language of Saint Paul was to me the true gate of Paradise.[2]

Luther called Romans "the chief part of the New Testament and the very purest gospel." He believed that "every Christian should know it word for word, by heart, [and] occupy himself with it every day, as the daily bread of his soul."[3]

Samuel Taylor Coleridge, the English poet, called Romans "the profoundest book in existence." The great Swiss commentator F. Godet wrote that in all probability "every great spiritual revival in the church will be connected as effect and cause with a deeper understanding of this book."[4]

Foundational Christianity

But are these statements really true? We live in a skeptical age, and it is not unreasonable to think that a sizable percentage of people hearing or reading such statements in our day will challenge them. We know that God used Romans 13:13–14 to change the life of St. Augustine, who altered history by his influence on the church of the Middle Ages. We know that God used Martin Luther to launch the Reformation. But that was long ago. Augustine lived in the fourth and fifth centuries. Luther labored in the fifteen hundreds. Times have changed since then. Is there any reason to expect a corresponding impact from a study of this ancient letter today?

There is every reason to expect it, and the chief reason is that *Christianity has been the most powerful, transforming force in human history, and the book of Romans is the most basic, most comprehensive statement of true Christianity.*

Not everyone has agreed with this assessment, of course. At times one teacher or another has been enamored with the so-called simple teachings of Jesus and has rejected the writings of Paul as too doctrinaire, too technical, or too harsh. All we really need to do is tell people God loves them, these instructors have said. Others have maintained that it is not what we believe that matters as much as what we do. According to this perspective, the social teachings of Christianity are the heart of Christianity. Doctrines divide, whereas ethics ennoble our lives and unite us.

These views have a seed of wisdom, but they overlook the major issue. The fundamental human problem is not to understand what proper behavior is; generally we know that quite well. The problem is that we do not do what we know we should do. Indeed, we even seem incapable of doing it. This is what Augustine discovered when he tried to reform his life apart from the power of Christ. Again, the problem is not that we need to know God loves us, though we often doubt that he does. Our hang-up is that we do not love God, as Luther, the pious monk, discovered. We are at war with God. In effect, we hate him; at the very least, we do not want him to rule over our lives and resent any meaningful attempts he makes to do so.

Romans shows how God deals with this problem. And because it tells how God deals with this basic dilemma of human life, it necessarily also unveils the true solution to nearly everything else. When we repent of our sin and thus truly come to love God, we discover the secret to an upright and satisfying life, and we become a power for good rather than a disruptive, downward force or merely an indifferent presence in society.

Here is an overview of the entire letter to guide your reading.

Section 1: Justification by Faith (Chapters 1–4)

A preliminary personal word and introduction (1:1–15). Romans is a doctrinal treatise placed between the opening and closing sections of a typical ancient letter. But unlike most ancient writers, Paul uses the opening section to introduce the theme that will occupy him at length later on: "the gospel of God." Gospel means "good news." Paul is announcing news that is not only good but superlatively good, since it comes from the one who is the great Good of all.

A brief statement of the theme (1:16–17). In his introduction Paul shows that the gospel centers on the person of God's Son, the Lord Jesus Christ. But what is this Good News specifically? Paul's short statement shows that it concerns God's righteousness freely given. These verses transformed the life of Martin Luther, for they showed that the answer to life comes not by striving to do good works to please God but by resting in the finished work of God for us in Jesus Christ.

An analysis of the depravity of human beings and an explanation of the work of Christ as the provision for that need (1:18–4:25). This is the first major section of the letter, and it contains the most penetrating and perceptive analysis of human nature in its relationship to God ever written. The first thing Paul shows is that, although people have knowledge of the existence of God through nature, all act as if the true God does not exist. Or if they acknowledge him verbally, they nevertheless distort their understanding so that they actually worship the creation rather than the Creator. God has not overlooked this willful ignorance, for he has punished it by abandoning people to the natural outworking of their sins.

17

This outworking of sin drags the race downward and enslaves us in invisible chains.

All are involved in this tragedy. The pagan is involved, for the moral disintegration of his life shows that he is held in sin's power. The "moral" individual is also involved, for although he approves of higher behavioral standards, he inevitably fails to live up to those standards. His guilt is even greater than the pagan's. Last of all, Paul unveils the need of the pious, or "religious," individual. The problem with the merely religious person is that the practice of religion alone cannot change the heart.

But here is where the gospel enters in. Although all are enmeshed in sin's tentacles—so that Paul can remind us, quoting from the Old Testament, that "'there is no one righteous, not even one; there is no one who understands, no one who seeks God. All have turned away, they have together become worthless; there is no one who does good, not even one'" (Rom. 3:10–12)—God took the initiative to save us. Through the work of Christ he provided the righteousness we lack, and he did this not only for Jews, who might have expected it, but also for Gentiles. This is why the late Welsh preacher D. Martyn Lloyd-Jones of London, England, calls Romans 3:21–31, in which this doctrine is stated, "one of the greatest and noblest statements in the whole realm of scripture."[5]

In Romans 4, which is also part of this section, Paul shows that the gospel he explained in chapter 3 has *always* been God's way of saving sinners. It is true that God accomplished salvation through the work of Jesus Christ, who from the perspective of Paul had lived in the not-far-distant past. But the timing is unimportant, says the apostle. Those who lived before Christ were saved by faith by looking forward to his coming, just as we who came afterward are saved by faith as we look back. Paul proves this by Old Testament statements concerning the patriarch Abraham and King David.

Section 2: The Reign of Grace (Chapters 5–8)

A review of the great scope of salvation (5:1–8:39). Lloyd-Jones is surely right when he suggests that in this section Paul is "showing . . . the certainty, fullness and finality"[6] of what God has done. This section includes sanctification, but the author is actually covering the full scope of what God's work in Christ means for the believer. It gives him a new status before God and new privileges (5:1–11). It joins him to the living Lord Jesus Christ, from whom flows a new life of righteousness (5:12–6:23). It releases him from the anguish of trying to attain to moral rectitude by law (7:1–25). It provides victory over sin by the power of the Holy Spirit (8:1–17). It ends in glorification, for nothing in heaven or earth can ever separate us from the inexpressible love and power of God in Jesus Christ (8:18–39).

Section 3: God and History (Chapters 9–11)

A Christian view of history (9:1–11:36). Chapters 9 through 11 are a continuation of everything said thus far, particularly Paul's treatment of the believer's eternal security in Christ, with which chapter 8 ends. Paul has argued that Jews and Gentiles alike are trapped by sin. He has shown that salvation is by Christ and that this salvation is eternal, beyond any possibility of repudiation by God. But, some might ask, what of God's ancient chosen people? Most Jews seem to have rejected Christ. If that is so, then one of two things must follow. Either (1) certain people can be saved without Christ (the Jews), which Paul has already said is impossible; or (2) salvation is not secure, since God has already apparently broken his covenant with the Jews and therefore should not be trusted.

Paul's answer is that God has not broken faith with Israel. On the contrary, he is doing today as he has always done.

God is utterly consistent. There was never a time in history when a Jew was saved just *because* that individual was a Jew. And no one is saved today merely by being what he or she is naturally: a churchgoer, a moral person, a philanthropist, an American (or any other nationality), or even a child of Christian parents. Salvation is by grace through faith, which means that it flows from God's choice and activity. It is God's salvation, after all, not man's. And God will work it out—he *is* working it out—until the fullness of his purpose regarding the salvation of a people for himself is complete.

This is the meaning of history. Its explanation is not found in the rise and fall of empires or in individual accomplishments. It is seen in God's choice of a people for himself and in his work of perfecting and eventually glorifying them. This thought is so wonderful to Paul that he ends this section of his letter (Rom. 11:33–36), with a tremendous doxology:

> Oh, the depth of the riches of the wisdom and
> knowledge of God!
> How unsearchable his judgments,
> and his paths beyond tracing out!
> "Who has known the mind of the Lord?
> Or who has been his counselor?"
> "Who has ever given to God,
> that God should repay him?"
> For from him and through him and to him are all
> things.
> To him be the glory forever! Amen.

Section 4: The New Humanity (Chapters 12–16)

The outworking of Christianity in individual and national life (12:1–15:13). Paul was no armchair theologian, no ivory-tower divine. His letters always contain and usually end with practical and personal considerations. It is the same here. Having explained the gospel of God's unmerited salvation in Christ and having answered all reasonable objections to it, Paul concludes by showing how the work of God inevitably spills over into the details of individual and national life. His point is not only that Christianity will make a difference in life—though it will—but also that it is the only thing that will ever actually make any true alteration in the world.

A conclusion embracing Paul's future plans and final greetings (15:14–16:27). Having begun in letter format, the apostle now ends the epistle in the same way. In this section he tells of his hopes for the church at Rome, unveils more of his plans to visit them after having first made a trip to Jerusalem with an offering for the Jewish saints, and sends greetings to Rome from the church at Corinth. Greetings from his fellow workers and a benediction end the letter.

Paul's Regular Teaching

In the nineteenth chapter of Acts, Luke the historian says that during Paul's missionary journeys, the apostle spent two years in Ephesus teaching "the word of the Lord" to all who lived in Asia (v. 10). A marginal note in one ancient manuscript suggests that he did this for five hours each day. Counting six days to each week and fifty-two weeks to each year, that makes 3,120 hours of apostolic instruction, considerably more than most bachelor or master of theology programs. What do you suppose Paul taught the residents of Asia during these two long years of instruction? I suggest he taught them essentially what he gave us in outline form in Romans: the ruin of the human race in sin and the provision of a perfect and eternal remedy for that ruin through the work of Jesus Christ. This is most likely what the apostle Paul would teach today if he were to work among us for the same length of time.

Is Romans relevant today? It is—as long as people of every race, culture, and nationality are estranged from God because of sin.

21

Is Christianity relevant? It is—as long as it can redeem us for God, produce holiness in those who are trapped by sin, explain the meaning of life, and change history.

As he drew near his initial summation of the epistle's teaching, Robert Haldane, the great nineteenth-century Scottish expositor of this letter, said:

> Paul, writing without any of the aids of human wisdom, draws his precepts from the fountain of heavenly truth, and inculcates on the disciples of Jesus a code of duties, which, if habitually practiced by mankind, would change the world from what it is—a scene of strife, jealousy and division—and make it what it was before the entrance of sin, a paradise fit for the Lord to visit and for man to dwell in.[7]

SECTION 1

Justification by Faith

Chapters 1–4

Part 1: Opening Statements

Romans 1:1–15

Paul, a servant of Christ Jesus, called to be an apostle and set apart for the gospel of God—the gospel he promised beforehand through his prophets in the Holy Scriptures regarding his Son, who as to his human nature was a descendant of David, and who through the Spirit of holiness was declared with power to be the Son of God by his resurrection from the dead: Jesus Christ our Lord. Through him and for his name's sake, we received grace and apostleship to call people from among all the Gentiles to the obedience that comes from faith. And you also are among those who are called to belong to Jesus Christ.

To all in Rome who are loved by God and called to be saints:

Grace and peace to you from God our Father and from the Lord Jesus Christ.

First, I thank my God through Jesus Christ for all of you, because your faith is being reported all over the world. God, whom I serve with my whole heart in preaching the gospel of his Son, is my witness how constantly I remember you in my prayers at all times; and I pray that now at last by God's will the way may be opened for me to come to you.

I long to see you so that I may impart to you some spiritual gift to make you strong—that is, that you and I may be mutually encouraged by each other's faith. I do not want you to be unaware, brothers, that I planned many times to come to you (but have been prevented from doing so until now) in order that I might have a harvest among you, just as I have had among the other Gentiles.

I am obligated both to Greeks and non-Greeks, both to the wise and the foolish. That is why I am so eager to preach the gospel also to you who are at Rome.

God's Grand Old Gospel

Set apart for the gospel of God.

ROMANS 1:1

The gospel is *God's* gospel. It is something God announced and accomplished and what *he* sent his apostles to proclaim. It is something God blesses and through which *he* saves men and women. The grammatical way of stating this is that the genitive ("of God") is a subjective rather than an objective genitive. It means that God creates and announces the gospel rather than that he is the object of its proclamation.

Note how prominent this point is in these early verses of Romans. God the Father has "promised [the gospel] beforehand through his prophets in the Holy Scriptures" (v. 2). He has sent his Son, the Lord Jesus Christ, to accomplish the work thus promised, with the result that the gospel, then as now, is "regarding" him (v. 3). Finally, it is "through him and for his name's sake" that Paul and the other apostles, exercising a calling received by them from God, were in the process of proclaiming the gospel to men and women everywhere (v. 5).

If God is concerned about his gospel to this extent, will he not bless it fully wherever these great truths are proclaimed?

27

Let me tell you one story of such a blessing. In the year 1816 a Scotsman by the name of Robert Haldane went to Switzerland. Haldane was a godly layman who, with his brother James Alexander, had been much used of the Lord in Scotland. In Geneva, on this particular occasion, he was sitting on a park bench in a garden in the open air and heard a group of young men talking. As he listened he realized two things. First, these were theological students. Second, they were ignorant of true Christianity. As a result of this encounter and after a few encouraging conversations, Haldane invited the students to his room and began to teach them the book of Romans. God honored this work, and the Holy Spirit blessed it by the conversions of these young men. They were converted one by one, and in turn they were instrumental in a religious revival that not only affected Switzerland but also spread to France and the Netherlands.

Why should it be any different today? If it were *our* gospel, we could expect nothing. But it is not our gospel. It is "the gospel of God," that grand old gospel that was "promised beforehand through his prophets in the Holy Scriptures" and achieved for us by the Lord Jesus Christ through his substitutionary death and resurrection. We should proclaim it fearlessly and with zeal, as did Paul.

Give thanks to God for his gospel. Pray now that as you read about the gospel in these devotions the Spirit will plant the truths of the gospel deep in your heart and help you proclaim those truths to others.

Part 2: The Heart of Biblical Religion

Romans 1:16–17

The Theme of the Epistle

For in the gospel a righteousness from God is revealed,
a righteousness that is by faith from first to last, just
as it is written: "The righteous will live by faith."

ROMANS 1:17

Paul tells of his experience of God's grace in Philippians. Paul had been an exceedingly moral man: "If anyone else thinks he has reasons to put confidence in the flesh, I have more: circumcised on the eighth day, of the people of Israel, of the tribe of Benjamin, a Hebrew of Hebrews; in regard to the law, a Pharisee; as for zeal, persecuting the church; as for legalistic righteousness, faultless" (Phil. 3:4–6). But Paul learned to count his attainments as nothing in order to have Christ "and be found in him, not having a righteousness of my own that comes from the law, but that which is through faith in Christ—the righteousness that comes from God and is by faith" (v. 9). This is a vivid, personal statement of what he also declares at the beginning of Romans.

In Philippians, Paul uses a helpful metaphor, saying that before he met Christ his thoughts about religion involved something like a lifelong balance sheet showing assets and liabilities. He had thought that being saved meant having more in the column of assets than in the column of liabilities. And since he had considerable assets, he felt he was very well-off indeed. Some assets he had inherited; some assets he had earned for himself. These were great assets from a human point of view. But the day came when God revealed his own righteousness to Paul in the person of Jesus Christ. When Paul saw Jesus he understood for the first time what real righteousness was. Moreover, he saw that what he had been calling righteousness, his *own* righteousness, was not righteousness at all but only filthy rags. It was no asset. It was actually a liability, because it had been keeping him from Jesus, where true righteousness alone could be found.

Mentally Paul moved his long list of cherished assets to the column of liabilities—for that is what they really were—and under assets he wrote "Jesus Christ alone." When those who have been made alive by God turn from their own attempts at righteousness, which can only condemn them, and instead embrace the Lord Jesus Christ by saving faith, God declares their sins to have been punished in Christ and imputes his own perfect righteousness to their account.

Make your own list of "assets"—raised in church, good works, generous donations, etc. Now move those "assets" over to the liabilities column and write "Jesus Christ alone" under assets. Thank God for that perfect righteousness that Jesus alone provides.

Part 3: The Race in Ruin

Romans 1:18–3:20

The wrath of God is being revealed from heaven against all the godlessness and wickedness of men who suppress the truth by their wickedness, since what may be known about God is plain to them, because God has made it plain to them. For since the creation of the world God's invisible qualities—his eternal power and divine nature—have been clearly seen, being understood from what has been made, so that men are without excuse.

For although they knew God, they neither glorified him as God nor gave thanks to him, but their thinking became futile and their foolish hearts were darkened. Although they claimed to be wise, they became fools and exchanged the glory of the immortal God for images made to look like mortal man and birds and animals and reptiles.

Therefore God gave them over in the sinful desires of their hearts to sexual impurity for the degrading of their bodies with one another. They exchanged the truth of God for a lie, and worshiped and served created things rather than the Creator—who is forever praised. Amen.

Because of this, God gave them over to shameful lusts. Even their women exchanged natural relations for unnatural ones. In the same way the men also abandoned natural relations with women and were inflamed with lust for one another. Men committed indecent acts with other men, and received in themselves the due penalty for their perversion.

Furthermore, since they did not think it worthwhile to retain the knowledge of God, he gave them over to a depraved mind, to do what ought not to be done. They have become filled with every kind of wickedness, evil, greed and depravity. They are full of envy, murder, strife, deceit and malice. They are gossips, slanderers, God-haters, insolent, arrogant and boastful; they invent ways of doing evil; they disobey their parents; they are senseless, faithless, heartless, ruthless. Although they know God's righteous decree that those who do such things deserve death, they not only continue to do these very things but also approve of those who practice them.

The Angry God

The wrath of God is being revealed from heaven
against all the godlessness and wickedness of men.

ROMANS 1:18

Where do most people begin when making a presentation of Christian truth? Many begin with what is often called "a felt need," a lack or a longing the listener will acknowledge. The need may involve feelings of inadequacy; a recognition of problems in the individual's personal relationships, work, or aspirations; moods; fears; or simply bad habits.

Here is the way Paul speaks of a felt need in another letter: "For the time will come when men will not put up with sound doctrine. Instead, to suit their own desires, they will gather around them a great number of teachers to say what their itching ears want to hear" (2 Tim. 4:3). "What their itching ears want to hear" is a classic example of a felt need. In this passage the apostle warns Timothy not to cater to it. Another way we present the gospel today is by promises. Through this approach, becoming a Christian is basically presented as a means of getting something. We also commonly offer the gospel by the route of personal experience, stressing what Jesus has done for us and commending the gospel to the other person for that reason.

The point I am making is that Paul does not do this in Romans, and in this matter he rebukes us profitably. Paul was God-centered rather than man-centered, and he was concerned with that central focus. Most of us are weak, fuzzy, or wrong at this point. Paul knew that what matters in the final analysis is not whether we feel good or have our felt needs met or receive a meaningful experience. What matters is whether we come into a right relationship with God. And to have that happen we need to begin with the truth that we are not in a right relationship with him. On the contrary, we are under God's wrath and are in danger of everlasting condemnation at his hands.

Our hope, then, is in Jesus, the Son of God. His death was for those who deserve God's wrath. And his death was fully adequate, because Jesus did not need to die for his own sins—he was sinless—and because, being God, his act was of infinite magnitude.

The place to begin for salvation is not with your own good works, since you have none, but by knowing that you are an object of God's wrath and will perish in sin, unless you throw yourself on the mercy of the one who died for sinners, even Jesus Christ.

What concerns you more—where you stand with God or how well you feel your life is going? Take this matter now before the Lord in prayer.

You, therefore, have no excuse, you who pass judgment on someone else, for at whatever point you judge the other, you are condemn-
ing yourself, because you who pass judgment do the same things. Now
we know that God's judgment against those who do such things is
based on truth. So when you, a mere man, pass judgment on them
and yet do the same things, do you think you will escape God's
judgment? Or do you show contempt for the riches of his kindness,
tolerance and patience, not realizing that God's kindness leads you
toward repentance?

But because of your stubbornness and your unrepentant heart,
you are storing up wrath against yourself for the day of God's wrath,
when his righteous judgment will be revealed. God "will give to each
person according to what he has done." To those who by persistence
in doing good seek glory, honor and immortality, he will give eternal
life. But for those who are self-seeking and who reject the truth and
follow evil, there will be wrath and anger. There will be trouble
and distress for every human being who does evil: first for the Jew,
then for the Gentile; but glory, honor and peace for everyone who
does good: first for the Jew, then for the Gentile. For God does not
show favoritism.

All who sin apart from the law will also perish apart from the
law, and all who sin under the law will be judged by the law. For it is
not those who hear the law who are righteous in God's sight, but it
is those who obey the law who will be declared righteous. (Indeed,
when Gentiles, who do not have the law, do by nature things required
by the law, they are a law for themselves, even though they do not
have the law, since they show that the requirements of the law are
written on their hearts, their consciences also bearing witness, and
their thoughts now accusing, now even defending them.) This will
take place on the day when God will judge men's secrets through
Jesus Christ, as my gospel declares.

The Long-Suffering God

Or do you show contempt for the riches of his kind-
ness, tolerance and patience, not realizing that
God's kindness leads you toward repentance?

ROMANS 2:4

There are two ways we can go in responding to God's kindness, tolerance, and patience. Paul is clear about them. One
way is repentance, the way Scripture urges. The other is defi-
ance, or spite toward God's goodness.

Which will it be for you? You can defy God. You can set
yourself against his goodness, tolerance, and patience. But
why should you do that? Why should you "show contempt
for the riches of his kindness, tolerance and patience"? These
are winsome qualities. A kind, tolerant, and patient God is a
good God. Why should you fail to realize that God's exercise
of these attributes toward you is for a good end?

I want to give you three reasons why you should allow these
attributes to lead you to repentance and should no longer
despise the goodness of God.

First, if God is a good God, then whatever you may think
to the contrary in your fallen state, to find this good God
will mean finding all good for yourself. You do not normally
think this way. You think that your own will is the good. Can

you not see that it is your own sinful way that is the cause of your miseries? God is not the cause. God is the source of all good. If you want to find good for yourself, the way to find it is to turn from whatever is holding you back and find God. God has provided the way for you to turn to him through the death of his Son, the Lord Jesus Christ.

Second, if God is tolerant of you, it is because he has a will to save you. If he wanted to condemn you outright, he could have done it long ago. If he is tolerant, you will find that if you come to him he will not cast you out.

Third, if God is patient with you in spite of your many follies, it is because he is giving you an opportunity to be saved. The apostle Peter wrote, "The Lord is not slow in keeping his promise, as some understand slowness. He is patient with you, not wanting anyone to perish, but everyone to come to repentance" (2 Peter 3:9). If God is good in his patience, his reason for being so must be to do good. His patience must be to give you opportunity to turn to him. If he has allowed you to live twenty, forty, or even eighty or ninety years, it is so that you might come to him now—before you die and the opportunity for salvation is gone forever.

Here is your opportunity to call upon God. Whether you have strayed from your early faith or never before turned to God, now is the time to repent and believe in the work of Christ that saves you.

Now you, if you call yourself a Jew; if you rely on the law and brag about your relationship to God; if you know his will and approve of what is superior because you are instructed by the law; if you are convinced that you are a guide for the blind, a light for those who are in the dark, an instructor of the foolish, a teacher of infants, because you have in the law the embodiment of knowledge and truth—you, then, who teach others, do you not teach yourself? You who preach against stealing, do you steal? You who say that people should not commit adultery, do you commit adultery? You who abhor idols, do you rob temples? You who brag about the law, do you dishonor God by breaking the law? As it is written: "God's name is blasphemed among the Gentiles because of you."

Circumcision has value if you observe the law, but if you break the law, you have become as though you had not been circumcised. If those who are not circumcised keep the law's requirements, will they not be regarded as though they were circumcised? The one who is not circumcised physically and yet obeys the law will condemn you who, even though you have the written code and circumcision, are a lawbreaker.

A man is not a Jew if he is only one outwardly, nor is circumcision merely outward and physical. No, a man is a Jew if he is one inwardly; and circumcision is circumcision of the heart, by the Spirit, not by the written code. Such a man's praise is not from men, but from God.

The Second Excuse: Religion

You who brag about the law, do you dis-
honor God by breaking the law?

ROMANS 2:23

Earlier in the chapter Paul addressed the excuse that the so-called moral person might give as to why he would not be under God's wrath. Let's imagine, now, how the religious person might respond to Paul describing the pagan morality of his day. "I am glad you have spoken as you have," this person might tell Paul, "because things really are in a terrible state today. God will certainly judge all these wicked people severely. So preach to them. But leave me out of it! I am a very religious person, and my religious commitments exempt me from your blanket condemnations. I have been a churchgoing person all my life. I have been baptized and confirmed. I go to communion. I give to the church's support."

Paul replies that these are genuinely good things and not to be ignored. "But you still need the gospel," he says.

"Why?"

"Because God is not interested in outward things alone—things like church membership, the sacraments, stewardship—but rather in what is within."

God says, "Man looks at the outward appearance, but the LORD looks at the heart" (1 Sam. 16:7).

Paul has been describing in verses 17–23 the true state of the orthodox, or "religious," person. He ends the paragraph by quoting the Old Testament to show that "God's name is blasphemed among the Gentiles because of you" (v. 24; cf. Isa. 52:5; Ezek. 36:22). This is always the case when ostensibly devout persons violate the very standards they proclaim. It is a terrible thing!

But there is something even more terrible, and that is for these same persons to continue nevertheless along this wrong path, supposing that they are on the best of standings with God—just because they are religious—when actually they are, like the utter pagans around them, on a swift journey to destruction.

If you have been trusting in *anything* other than Jesus Christ and his death on the cross in your place, throw whatever it is completely out of your mind. Abandon it. Stamp on it. Grind it down. Dust off the place where it lay.

Then turn to Jesus Christ alone and trust him only.

Have you been trusting in your good works or religious practices to shield you from God's judgment?

What advantage, then, is there in being a Jew, or what value is there in circumcision? Much in every way! First of all, they have been entrusted with the very words of God.

What if some did not have faith? Will their lack of faith nullify God's faithfulness? Not at all! Let God be true, and every man a liar. As it is written:

> "So that you may be proved right when you
> speak
> and prevail when you judge."

But if our unrighteousness brings out God's righteousness more clearly, what shall we say? That God is unjust in bringing his wrath on us? (I am using a human argument.) Certainly not! If that were so, how could God judge the world? Someone might argue, "If my falsehood enhances God's truthfulness and so increases his glory, why am I still condemned as a sinner?" Why not say—as we are being slanderously reported as saying and as some claim that we say—"Let us do evil that good may result"? Their condemnation is deserved.

What shall we conclude then? Are we any better? Not at all! We have already made the charge that Jews and Gentiles alike are all under sin. As it is written:

> "There is no one righteous, not even one;
>   there is no one who understands,
>   no one who seeks God.
> All have turned away,
>   they have together become worthless;
> there is no one who does good,
>   not even one."
> "Their throats are open graves;
>   their tongues practice deceit."
> "The poison of vipers is on their lips."
>   "Their mouths are full of cursing and
>   bitterness."
> "Their feet are swift to shed blood;
>   ruin and misery mark their ways,
> and the way of peace they do not know."
>   "There is no fear of God before their eyes."

Now we know that whatever the law says, it says to those who are under the law, so that every mouth may be silenced and the whole world held accountable to God. Therefore no one will be declared righteous in his sight by observing the law; rather, through the law we become conscious of sin.

Silence at Last

Now we know that whatever the law says, it says to those who are under the law, so that every mouth may be silenced and the whole world held accountable to God.

ROMANS 3:19

Some years ago a dance instructor had been out late on a Saturday evening. In the wee hours of the morning he staggered back to his hotel room, fell into bed, and went to sleep. The next morning he was suddenly jolted awake by his clock radio. A man was speaking, and he was asking this question: "If in the next few moments some great disaster should happen and you should be killed, and if you should find yourself before God and he should ask you, 'What right do you have to come into my heaven?' what would you say?"

The dance instructor was amazed and confounded by this question. He realized that he did not have an answer. He had not a single thing to say. He sat silently on the edge of his bed as Donald Grey Barnhouse explained the answer to him. That dance instructor was D. James Kennedy, author of the evangelism program known as "Evangelism Explosion." Kennedy believed in Jesus Christ that day, and the question that had been used to save him became the chief tool in his evangelism strategy.

I ask that same question of you. Someday you will die. You will face God, and he will say to you, "What right do you have to come into my heaven?" What will your response be?

Perhaps you will say, "Well, here is my record. I know I have done some bad things, but I have done a lot of good things too. All I want from you is justice." If you say that, justice is exactly what you will get. You will be judged for your sin and condemned. Your good works will not save you, for as we have seen, God has said, "There is no one righteous, not even one" (Rom. 3:10).

Perhaps you will not plead your good works but instead will stand before God silenced. This is better. At least you will have recognized that your goodness is not adequate before God. You will know you are a sinner. But it is still a most pitiful position to be in: silent before the one great Judge of the universe, with no possibility of making a defense, no possibility of urging extenuating circumstances, no hope of escaping condemnation.

So what will you say? I trust you will be able to answer, "My right to heaven is the Lord Jesus Christ. He died for me. He took the punishment for my sin. He is my right to heaven, because he has become my righteousness."

You stand before God and he asks you now, "What right do you have to come into my heaven?" What answer can you give?

Part 4: God's Remedy in Christ

Romans 3:21–31

But now a righteousness from God, apart from law, has been made known, to which the Law and the Prophets testify. This righteousness from God comes through faith in Jesus Christ to all who believe. There is no difference, for all have sinned and fall short of the glory of God, and are justified freely by his grace through the redemption that came by Christ Jesus. God presented him as a sacrifice of atonement, through faith in his blood. He did this to demonstrate his justice, because in his forbearance he had left the sins committed beforehand unpunished—he did it to demonstrate his justice at the present time, so as to be just and the one who justifies those who have faith in Jesus.

Amazing Grace

*And are justified freely by his grace through
the redemption that came by Christ Jesus.*

ROMANS 3:24

When a person is first presented with the pure core of Christianity, the reaction is usually revulsion. We want to save ourselves, and anything that suggests we cannot do so is abhorrent to us. But Christianity is not only the religion we *need* so desperately, it is also the only religion *worth having* in the long run. Let me explain.

If salvation is by the gift of God, apart from human doing, then we can be saved now. We do not have to wait until we reach some high level of attainment or pass some undetermined future test. Many people think in these terms, because they know that their lives and actions are far from what they should be now and they keep striving. But this means that salvation can never be a present experience but is something always in the future. It is something such persons hope to attain, though they are afraid they may not. It is only in Christianity that this future element moves into the present, because of what God has *already* done for us in Christ.

If salvation is by the gift of God, apart from human doing, then salvation is certain. If salvation is by human works, then human works (or a lack of them) can undo it. If I can save myself, I can unsave myself. I can ruin everything. But if salvation is of God from beginning to end, it is sure and unwavering simply because God is himself sure and unwavering. What he has begun he will continue, and we can be confident of that.

If salvation is by the gift of God, apart from human doing, then human boasting is excluded, and all the glory in salvation goes to God. I doubt any of us would want to be in a heaven populated by persons who got there, even in part, by their own efforts. The boasting of human beings is bad enough in this world, where all they have to boast about are their good looks, their money, their friends, or whatever. Imagine how offensive it would be if they were able to brag about having earned heaven through works, even the work of faith.

But it is not going to be like that! Salvation is a gift. It is receiving God's righteousness—apart from law, apart from human doing. It is, as Paul wrote to the Ephesians, "not by works, so that no one can boast" (2:9). No one in heaven will be praising man. In heaven the glory will go to God only. *Soli deo gloria!*

Thank God it is that way.

Take time now to thank God that because salvation is wholly from him, your salvation is effective now, it is secure, and to him alone belongs all the glory.

50

Where, then, is boasting? It is excluded. On what principle? On that of observing the law? No, but on that of faith. For we maintain that a man is justified by faith apart from observing the law. Is God the God of Jews only? Is he not the God of Gentiles too? Yes, of Gentiles too, since there is only one God, who will justify the circumcised by faith and the uncircumcised through that same faith. Do we, then, nullify the law by this faith? Not at all! Rather, we uphold the law.

One Way for Everybody

Since there is only one God, who will jus-
tify the circumcised by faith and the uncir-
cumcised through that same faith.

ROMANS 3:30

I want to tell you that whoever you are or whatever you may or may not have done, the gospel is for you, because *it is for everybody.* I want you to see that if you come to God in the way he has appointed for you to come—that is, through faith in his Son, the Lord Jesus Christ, who died for you—he will receive you and will never cast you out.

Who may come? The answer is: everybody. All alike are lost in sin, and yet all alike are the objects of Jesus's saving love. The gospel is for the very great sinner as well as for the apparently moral person. It is for the pagan as well as for the one who considers himself or herself religious. Even if you are a very great sinner, you may come. Even if you are extremely self-righteous, you may come—if you shed your self-righteousness.

What is your sin? Pride? Murder? Stealing? Adultery? It does not matter. If you come to Jesus, you will be received. Jesus said, "Whoever comes to me I will never drive away" (John 6:37).

What is your profession? Minister? Gambler? Business-man? Housewife? It does not matter. You may come to God through faith in the atoning work of Jesus Christ.

What is your condition? Are you seeking God? Running away from God? Fighting God? Questioning God? Job questioned God, but God was never closer to him than when he was questioning.

How may I come? You may come as you are. You are invited to come to Christ in whatever mental or spiritual attire you may find yourself in. Some come running to Jesus. Others come limping along with poor, faltering, hesitating steps. Some people come kicking and screaming. But that is all right. They may come too.

When may I come? You may come at any time. Come as a child. Jesus commended the faith of children, saying that we must all come as little children to be saved. You may be older. You may be thinking that you probably should have come as a child and it is too late for you now. It is never too late. You may not be able to do much for Jesus because of your advanced years, but he can do everything for you. You will not have much time on earth to serve him, but you will have an eternity in heaven to praise him.

Have you come to Jesus? Have you strayed and need to return? Come now to him while you can. It is not too late. Just come.

Part 5: The Gospel Proved from Scripture

Romans 4:1–25

What then shall we say that Abraham, our forefather, discovered in this matter? If, in fact, Abraham was justified by works, he had something to boast about—but not before God. What does the Scripture say? "Abraham believed God, and it was credited to him as righteousness."

Now when a man works, his wages are not credited to him as a gift, but as an obligation. However, to the man who does not work but trusts God who justifies the wicked, his faith is credited as righteousness. David says the same thing when he speaks of the blessedness of the man to whom God credits righteousness apart from works:

> "Blessed are they
>   whose transgressions are forgiven,
>   whose sins are covered.
> Blessed is the man
>   whose sin the Lord will never count against
>   him."

Is this blessedness only for the circumcised, or also for the uncircumcised? We have been saying that Abraham's faith was credited to him as righteousness. Under what circumstances was it credited? Was it after he was circumcised, or before? It was not after, but before! And he received the sign of circumcision, a seal of the righteousness that he had by faith while he was still uncircumcised. So then, he is the father of all who believe but have not been circumcised, in order that righteousness might be credited to them. And he is also the father of the circumcised who not only are circumcised but who also walk in the footsteps of the faith that our father Abraham had before he was circumcised.

It was not through law that Abraham and his offspring received the promise that he would be heir of the world, but through the righteousness that comes by faith. For if those who live by law are heirs, faith has no value and the promise is worthless, because law brings wrath. And where there is no law there is no transgression.

David's Testimony

Blessed is the man whose sin the Lord
will never count against him.

ROMANS 4:8

There is a word in Paul's citation of David's testimony that deserves special consideration. It is the word *never*, which occurs in the sentence, "Blessed is the man whose sin the Lord will *never* count against him."

Never means never, and it must be taken at full value here, even though the opposite is almost always the case in human relationships. We all know the kind of forgiveness in which a person reluctantly accepts our apology and says he will forgive us. But we know as he says this that he is not forgetting what happened, that our offense will linger in his mind and will probably be brought out against us in the future.

This text tells us that God is not like that. It tells us that once he has forgiven us for our sin through the work of Christ, he will *never, never* bring it up to us again. He will not bring it up in this life, never remind us of something in the past. He will always begin with us precisely where we are in the present. And he will never bring it up at the day of judgment. Why? Because it is truly forgiven. It will *never* be remembered anymore.

That is real "blessedness," which is the terminology David uses. And so my question is this: Why trade away that blessedness for the false blessings offered by this world?

The world does offer its blessings, of course. It is how it holds its victims. It offers material things chiefly, but it also offers intangibles such as a good reputation, success, happiness, and so on. Let me remind you that you can have all these things and more and still be miserable—if the burden of your sin is not lifted. David is an example. He was the king of a most favored nation. He had wealth and reputation. But the very psalm from which the verses we have been studying are taken describes what he was like before his sin was forgiven. He wrote that when he kept silent about his sin, trying to hush it up, "my bones wasted away through my groaning all day long. For day and night your hand was heavy upon me; my strength was sapped as in the heat of summer" (Ps. 32:3–4). But because David found forgiveness with God, the burden of his sin rolled away, his strength was restored, and he could write, "Blessed is the man whose sin the Lord will never count against him."

I commend that very great blessing to you.

Why trade away that blessed forgiveness for the false blessings offered by this world? And why, if you have received this blessing, act as though God still counts your sin against you? Take God at his word—never will your sin be brought up again. Thank him now for such blessing.

Therefore, the promise comes by faith, so that it may be by grace and may be guaranteed to all Abraham's offspring—not only to those who are of the law but also to those who are of the faith of Abraham. He is the father of us all. As it is written: "I have made you a father of many nations." He is our father in the sight of God, in whom he believed—the God who gives life to the dead and calls things that are not as though they were.

Against all hope, Abraham in hope believed and so became the father of many nations, just as it had been said to him, "So shall your offspring be." Without weakening in his faith, he faced the fact that his body was as good as dead—since he was about a hundred years old—and that Sarah's womb was also dead. Yet he did not waver through unbelief regarding the promise of God, but was strengthened in his faith and gave glory to God, being fully persuaded that God had power to do what he had promised. This is why "it was credited to him as righteousness." The words "it was credited to him" were written not for him alone, but also for us, to whom God will credit righteousness—for us who believe in him who raised Jesus our Lord from the dead. He was delivered over to death for our sins and was raised to life for our justification.

The Christian Faith

*The words "it was credited to him" were writ-
ten not for him alone, but also for us, to whom God
will credit righteousness—for us who believe in
him who raised Jesus our Lord from the dead.*

ROMANS 4:23–24

Paul began Romans with an analysis of man's lost condition.
The human race is under the wrath of God for its failure to
receive the revelation of God that he has made in nature,
and its refusal to thank God for creation and to seek him
more fully in order to worship him. Instead of following
the truth, people have suppressed the truth, and in its place
they have created imaginary gods like themselves and even
like animals. Having turned from God, who is the source of
all good, they are on a downhill path, which they will follow
until they come at last to the point where they are willing to
call good evil, and evil good.

No one naturally agrees to this assessment, of course. It is
part of what rejecting truth is all about. So Paul next spends
time dealing with the arguments of those who exempt themselves from those conclusions, including the ethically moral
person and the religious person. The end of his argument is
that all stand condemned before God.

Finally, Paul unfolds the gospel, showing that God acted to save sinners through the Lord Jesus Christ. We cannot save ourselves. We do not deserve saving. But God is gracious, and because he is, he sent the Lord Jesus Christ to die in our place. By his death, Jesus turned the wrath of God aside and became the grounds on which God is able to justify the ungodly. At the end of Romans 4, Paul returns to this theme after having shown that this is the same method by which the Old Testament saints, such as Abraham, were justified.

Abraham was saved by faith. So the question is: Do you believe in God and trust his promises, as the patriarch did? Here is what Paul says about Abraham's faith: Abraham (1) believed God's promise; (2) believed on the basis of the Word of God only; (3) believed in spite of adverse circumstances; (4) was fully assured that God would do whatever he had promised; and (5) acted on that confidence.

That is what you must do too. God promises salvation through the work of Jesus Christ. You must trust his word in this. Abraham "did not waver through unbelief regarding the promise of God, but was strengthened in his faith and gave glory to God" (Rom. 4:20). Neither should your faith falter. Receive the promise, and believe in the God who raised Jesus our Lord from the dead.

Do you believe in God and trust his promise of salvation through the work of Jesus Christ? To believe in God you must first believe God. Speak to him now about trusting him.

The Reign of Grace

Chapters 5–8

Part 6: Security in Christ

Romans 5:1–11

Therefore, since we have been justified through faith, we have peace with God through our Lord Jesus Christ, through whom we have gained access by faith into this grace in which we now stand. And we rejoice in the hope of the glory of God. Not only so, but we also rejoice in our sufferings, because we know that suffering produces perseverance; perseverance, character; and character, hope. And hope does not disappoint us, because God has poured out his love into our hearts by the Holy Spirit, whom he has given us.

You see, at just the right time, when we were still powerless, Christ died for the ungodly. Very rarely will anyone die for a righteous man, though for a good man someone might possibly dare to die. But God demonstrates his own love for us in this: While we were still sinners, Christ died for us.

Since we have now been justified by his blood, how much more shall we be saved from God's wrath through him! For if, when we were God's enemies, we were reconciled to him through the death of his Son, how much more, having been reconciled, shall we be saved through his life! Not only is this so, but we also rejoice in God through our Lord Jesus Christ, through whom we have now received reconciliation.

God's Love Commended

But God demonstrates his own love for us in this:
While we were still sinners, Christ died for us.

ROMANS 5:8

How can any merely human words sufficiently express the greatness of God's love for us? Did you know that the love of God seemed so great to the biblical writers that they invented, or at least raised to an entirely new level of meaning, a brand-new word for love?

The Greek language was rich in words for love. There was the word *storgē*, which referred to affection, particularly within the family. There was *philia*, from which we get "philharmonic" and "philanthropy" and "Philadelphia." It refers to a love between friends. A third word was *erōs*, which has given us "erotic," and which referred to sexual love. This was a rich linguistic heritage. Yet, when the Old Testament was translated into Greek and when the New Testament writers later wrote in Greek, they found that none of these common Greek words was able to express what they wanted. They therefore took another word without strong associations and poured their own, biblical meaning into it. The new word was *agapē*, which thereby came to mean the holy, gracious, sovereign, everlasting, and giving love of God that is expressed here.

If you do not yet fully appreciate (or perhaps have not even begun to appreciate) the greatness of the love God has for you, the explanation is probably that you have never really thought of yourself as God saw you in your fallen state.

Perhaps you have never thought of yourself as someone who was utterly without strength or powerless before God saved you.

Perhaps you have never considered yourself to have been ungodly.

Nor a sinner.

Nor God's enemy.

But that is what you were—and still are if you have never come to Christ in order to be justified. It is only if you can recognize the truth of these descriptions that you can begin to appreciate the love God holds out to you through the death of his Son.

If you have never responded to this great overture of the divine love, let me encourage you to do that, assuring you that there is no greater truth in all the universe. Can you think of anything greater? Of course, you can't. How could anybody? God loves you. Jesus died for you. Let those truly great thoughts move you to abandon your sin, love God in return, and live for Jesus.

> To understand God's love is to understand that you do not deserve it. Can you admit that? As painful as the admission may be, to grasp this undeserving love of God is a great blessing. Take time now to open your heart before your Father about your sin and to receive his love.

Part 7: Union with Jesus Christ

Romans 5:12–6:23

Therefore, just as sin entered the world through one man, and death through sin, and in this way death came to all men, because all sinned—for before the law was given, sin was in the world. But sin is not taken into account when there is no law. Nevertheless, death reigned from the time of Adam to the time of Moses, even over those who did not sin by breaking a command, as did Adam, who was a pattern of the one to come.

But the gift is not like the trespass. For if the many died by the trespass of the one man, how much more did God's grace and the gift that came by the grace of the one man, Jesus Christ, overflow to the many! Again, the gift of God is not like the result of the one man's sin: The judgment followed one sin and brought condemnation, but the gift followed many trespasses and brought justification. For if, by the trespass of the one man, death reigned through that one man, how much more will those who receive God's abundant provision of grace and of the gift of righteousness reign in life through the one man, Jesus Christ.

Consequently, just as the result of one trespass was condemnation for all men, so also the result of one act of righteousness was justification that brings life for all men. For just as through the disobedience of the one man the many were made sinners, so also through the obedience of the one man the many will be made righteous.

The law was added so that the trespass might increase. But where sin increased, grace increased all the more, so that, just as sin reigned in death, so also grace might reign through righteousness to bring eternal life through Jesus Christ our Lord.

Three Great Contrasts

*How much more will those who receive God's abun-
dant provision of grace and of the gift of righteousness
reign in life through the one man, Jesus Christ.*

ROMANS 5:17

Adam fell because he was not able by his own strength to
confirm himself in righteousness. Similarly, were we to attempt to stand in our own righteousness, assuming that we
could attain to it in the first place, we would fall also. But we
do not fall. We stand instead, and the reason we stand is that
we do not stand in our own righteousness. So we sing:

> Jesus *thy* Blood and righteousness
> My beauty are, my glorious dress;
> 'Midst flaming worlds in these arrayed,
> With joy shall I lift up my head.

Moreover, it is not only that we will stand in that final day
of divine judgment. We stand now, which is what the phrase
"reigning in life" refers to. It means that by the grace of the
Lord Jesus Christ, the love of God, and the communion and
empowering of the Holy Spirit, we are victorious *now*. In

this way the gift of God in Christ far surpasses the effects of Adam's and all other transgressions.

We were in Adam once, and we fell in him. What then? Good news! We can escape the effects of Adam's fall. More than that, we can rise above the position in which Adam first stood. We can stand in a divine righteousness, which is perfect and can never be taken away from us. It enables us to reign in life, triumphing over sin, as Adam, in his own human (though once perfect) righteousness, could not. Therefore we can sing:

> On Christ the solid rock I stand;
> All other ground is sinking sand.

Are you "in Jesus"? Adam was not "in Jesus," and he fell, even from his high pinnacle of human perfection. If he who was once humanly perfect fell, what chance do *you* have to stand, you who are corrupted by many sins and wholly disposed to unrighteousness? Your only hope is to believe on Jesus and be joined to him. It is to stand in him, as you originally stood (but also fell) in Adam.

Are you "in Jesus"? If so, whatever happens today, you will be upheld by him. Give him thanks. If not, then you will remain in your fallen state. The choice is before you. Call on him that you may be in him.

What shall we say, then? Shall we go on sinning so that grace may increase? By no means! We died to sin; how can we live in it any longer? Or don't you know that all of us who were baptized into Christ Jesus were baptized into his death? We were therefore buried with him through baptism into death in order that, just as Christ was raised from the dead through the glory of the Father, we too may live a new life.

If we have been united with him like this in his death, we will certainly also be united with him in his resurrection. For we know that our old self was crucified with him so that the body of sin might be done away with, that we should no longer be slaves to sin—because anyone who has died has been freed from sin.

Now if we died with Christ, we believe that we will also live with him. For we know that since Christ was raised from the dead, he cannot die again; death no longer has mastery over him. The death he died, he died to sin once for all; but the life he lives, he lives to God.

Where Do We Go from Here?

We died to sin; how can we live in it any longer?
ROMANS 6:2

A reigning monarch is a triumphant monarch. If grace is reigning in us, grace is advancing its conquest over sin. Christians sin. But they are not defeated by sin, and they do not continue in it.

Do you understand the absurdity of the objector's question: "Shall we go on sinning so that grace may increase?" If you understand the nature of grace, you will understand that for grace to increase, sin must decrease, not increase. The goal of grace is to destroy and vanquish sin. Therefore, if a person goes on sinning, as the objection suggests, it shows that he or she actually has no part in grace and is not saved.

I give two warnings.

The first is directed particularly to the many people in religious circles who have much head knowledge about doctrine and who suppose, just because they know such things and give mental assent to them, that all is therefore well with their souls and they are saved. That is not necessarily the case. If you are such a person, I need to warn you that it is not enough for you only to believe these things. Salvation is not mere knowledge. It is a new life. It is union with Christ.

Therefore, unless you are turning from sin and going on in righteousness, as you follow after Jesus Christ, you are not saved. It is presumptuous to believe you are. So examine your life. Make sure you are saved. The Bible warns you to "make your calling and election sure" (2 Peter 1:10).

The other warning is to all Christians, and it is in the words of an old Puritan preacher who asked in relation to our passage from Romans, "Is there anyone here who, by his conduct, gives occasion for this objection?"[1] Is your life so careless that an unsaved person looking on might reasonably conclude that this is precisely where the doctrine of justification by grace leads Christians?

If that is the case, correct that impression at once. The writer to whom I was referring says, "It is a lamentable fact that one man who dishonors the gospel by an unholy walk does more injury to the souls of men than ten holy ones can do them good."[2] I urge you to be part of the solution, part of the ten, rather than part of the problem. Let your life be marked by righteousness, not marred by sin—for your own soul's good as well as for the good of other people.

Do you let the doctrine of justification by grace excuse your sin? Examine your heart and let the grace of God move you to strive for righteousness.

In the same way, count yourselves dead to sin but alive to God in Christ Jesus. Therefore do not let sin reign in your mortal body so that you obey its evil desires. Do not offer the parts of your body to sin, as instruments of wickedness, but rather offer yourselves to God, as those who have been brought from death to life; and offer the parts of your body to him as instruments of righteousness. For sin shall not be your master, because you are not under law, but under grace.

What then? Shall we sin because we are not under law but under grace? By no means! Don't you know that when you offer yourselves to someone to obey him as slaves, you are slaves to the one whom you obey—whether you are slaves to sin, which leads to death, or to obedience, which leads to righteousness? But thanks be to God that, though you used to be slaves to sin, you wholeheartedly obeyed the form of teaching to which you were entrusted. You have been set free from sin and have become slaves to righteousness.

I put this in human terms because you are weak in your natural selves. Just as you used to offer the parts of your body in slavery to impurity and to ever-increasing wickedness, so now offer them in slavery to righteousness leading to holiness. When you were slaves to sin, you were free from the control of righteousness. What benefit did you reap at that time from the things you are now ashamed of? Those things result in death! But now that you have been set free from sin and have become slaves to God, the benefit you reap leads to holiness, and the result is eternal life. For the wages of sin is death, but the gift of God is eternal life in Christ Jesus our Lord.

Sin's Wages and God's Gift

*For the wages of sin is death, but the gift of God
is eternal life in Christ Jesus our Lord.*

ROMANS 6:23

Notice the phrase "in Christ Jesus our Lord." It brings out what was all-important to Paul, indeed the great truth for which the entire book of Romans was written. It is as if Paul stopped here and reflected: "I have said that salvation is the free gift of God. But surely I can't let it go at that. Salvation is the gift of God, yes! But how is it possible for God to be this gracious to us? How can he have given us the gift of eternal life, we being the sinners that we are?" The answer, of course, is that salvation is *by, in,* and *through* Jesus Christ. Paul never forgot that we are saved from sin only because of Jesus's work.

And that raises another question—a personal one, because religion always is personal; it must be. *Are you in Jesus?* Is Jesus your Savior, your Lord? There are only two ways you can answer that question, either yes or no. He either is your Savior or he is not.

If he is, let me ask these follow-up questions: Are you living for Jesus? If you are not, why not? He gave himself for you. He died for you. He even lives for you. If you are delivered from your bondage to sin by Jesus, it is so that you might thereafter be his, starting in this life.

The other way you can answer my question is no. And if that is the case, I ask why you would willingly keep going on such a self-destructive path, particularly when the way of salvation is known to you. Haven't you been trapped by sin long enough? Don't you long for deliverance?

I like the way Charles Haddon Spurgeon ended his sermon on this text. He referred to the question God asked the prophet Ezekiel when he stood in the Valley of Dry Bones. "Son of man, can these bones live?" (Ezek. 37:3). Ezekiel said, "O Sovereign LORD, you alone know." (We would have said, "Not likely!") But when he was told to preach to them he did, and those dry bones came together, took on flesh, rose up, and became a great army.

That is what is necessary if you are to be delivered from sin, says Spurgeon. The wages of sin is death, and spiritually speaking you are as dead as those dry bones in the valley. No one but God can bring life out of death. No one but Jesus can make your dead bones live. God can do it. And he will as you come to him. You need to come. You need to come now.

What is keeping you from coming to Jesus and living in him and for him? Is it temptation? Is it fear? Is it the consequences of sin? Confess whatever hinders you and see Jesus make your "dead bones" live.

Part 8: Freedom from Law

Romans 7:1–25

Do you not know, brothers—for I am speaking to men who know the law—that the law has authority over a man only as long as he lives? For example, by law a married woman is bound to her husband as long as he is alive, but if her husband dies, she is released from the law of marriage. So then, if she marries another man while her husband is still alive, she is called an adulteress. But if her husband dies, she is released from that law and is not an adulteress, even though she marries another man.

So, my brothers, you also died to the law through the body of Christ, that you might belong to another, to him who was raised from the dead, in order that we might bear fruit to God. For when we were controlled by the sinful nature, the sinful passions aroused by the law were at work in our bodies, so that we bore fruit for death. But now, by dying to what once bound us, we have been released from the law so that we serve in the new way of the Spirit, and not in the old way of the written code.

Our Second, Fruitful Union

*That you might belong to another, to him who was raised
from the dead, in order that we might bear fruit to God.*

ROMANS 7:4

God's object in saving us is *so that we, who beforehand were
lost in sin and wickedness, might live a holy life.* Our new
marriage to Jesus Christ produces holiness by bringing us into
a love that will never fade and a relationship that will never
end. We died to our unfruitful first marriage to the law when
we died in Christ. That marriage ended. But now, having been
raised in Christ, who will never die, and having been joined
to him, we are assured of a love that will last forever.

"But suppose my love is weak?" you ask.

Don't say "suppose." As a new bride of Christ, your love
for him *is* weak, but it will grow. It will grow here on earth,
and it will go on growing throughout eternity.

"Suppose my love should grow cold?" you wonder.

That is a sad thing to imagine since there is no excuse for
it, but it is true that this sometimes happens. We get involved
in the affairs of this world and forget the Lord for a time.
Ah, but he is still seeking us. He has only used our neglect
of him to show us how much his love means and how empty
our lives are without it.

81

"But suppose I betray his love, as Gomer betrayed the love of Hosea?" God forbid that you should ever do that! But even if that should happen, Jesus's love is greater even than your betrayal. He died to deliver you from the condemnation of the law and purchase you for himself. Do you think he will abandon you now? The Bible tells us, "If we are faithless, he will remain faithful, for he cannot disown himself" (2 Tim. 2:13).

One day the great God of the universe is going to throw a party. It will be the most magnificent party ever held. The banquet will be spread in heaven. The guests will be numbered in the billions. The angelic legions will be there to serve these honored guests. Jesus, the Bridegroom, will be seated at his Father's right hand. And you will be there too, for this is the great marriage supper of the Lamb. You will be there. Do you understand that? *You will be there.* Nothing is going to keep you from that great celebration—if you are really joined to Jesus Christ.

If you know where you are headed, you will prepare for that day with every spiritual thought you have and with every deed you do. You will bear fruit for God, because on that day of celebration you will be able to lift it up and offer it to him with pure hands and with joy unspeakable.

Is your hope set on this great banquet to come? How are you preparing for it in the way you are living today? Let us serve him with joyful expectation, eagerly looking forward to what he has so graciously prepared for us.

What shall we say, then? Is the law sin? Certainly not! Indeed I would not have known what sin was except through the law. For I would not have known what coveting really was if the law had not said, "Do not covet." But sin, seizing the opportunity afforded by the commandment, produced in me every kind of covetous desire. For apart from law, sin is dead. Once I was alive apart from law; but when the commandment came, sin sprang to life and I died. I found that the very commandment that was intended to bring life actually brought death. For sin, seizing the opportunity afforded by the commandment, deceived me, and through the commandment put me to death. So then, the law is holy, and the commandment is holy, righteous and good.

Did that which is good, then, become death to me? By no means! But in order that sin might be recognized as sin, it produced death in me through what was good, so that through the commandment sin might become utterly sinful.

We know that the law is spiritual; but I am unspiritual, sold as a slave to sin. I do not understand what I do. For what I want to do I do not do, but what I hate I do. And if I do what I do not want to do, I agree that the law is good. As it is, it is no longer I myself who do it, but it is sin living in me. I know that nothing good lives in me, that is, in my sinful nature. For I have the desire to do what is good, but I cannot carry it out. For what I do is not the good I want to do; no, the evil I do not want to do—this I keep on doing. Now if I do what I do not want to do, it is no longer I who do it, but it is sin living in me that does it.

So I find this law at work: When I want to do good, evil is right there with me. For in my inner being I delight in God's law; but I see another law at work in the members of my body, waging war against the law of my mind and making me a prisoner of the law of sin at work within my members. What a wretched man I am! Who will rescue me from this body of death? Thanks be to God—through Jesus Christ our Lord!

So then, I myself in my mind am a slave to God's law, but in the sinful nature a slave to the law of sin.

Victory through Jesus Christ Our Lord!

Thanks be to God—through Jesus Christ our Lord!
Romans 7:25

Although much of what Paul has written in Romans 7 sounds discouraging, it is not really discouraging at all. In fact, by contrast, there is enormous ground for genuine encouragement in what he says.

Chapter 5 speaks of the triumph of God's grace: "The law was added so that the trespass might increase. But where sin increased, grace increased all the more, so that, just as sin reigned in death, so also grace might reign through righteousness to bring eternal life through Jesus Christ our Lord" (Rom. 5:20–21).

"Through Jesus Christ our Lord." That is exactly the place to which we come at the end of chapter 7, and the point is the same. Victory is ours. The triumph of grace is assured, regardless of how badly we may think we are doing now or how near despair we may be due to the intensity or duration of the struggle. It is the very knowledge of a final victory that will enable us to fight on.

When the armies of Oliver Cromwell were winning battle after battle in the English Civil War, they believed they could not lose because they knew, even before they started to fight, that God had given them the victory. I do not know how true that was of Cromwell's army. Christians fought on both sides of that conflict, and Cromwell's cause was not entirely free of base motives. But whatever the case with Cromwell's soldiers in those very human battles, the principle does hold true for us, the soldiers of Jesus Christ who are engaged in fierce spiritual warfare against sin.

Apart from Jesus, not one of us can prevail for a moment. But united to him, we not only can prevail but will prevail. The Bible promises that "he who began a good work in [us] will carry it on to completion until the day of Christ Jesus" (Phil. 1:6).

And there is this too: Although your struggles may be prolonged and difficult, they are not essentially different from those of the many believers who have preceded you, including Paul and the other great personalities of Scripture. They triumphed, and so will you. Remember this text: "No temptation has seized you except what is common to man. And God is faithful; he will not let you be tempted beyond what you can bear. But when you are tempted, he will also provide a way out so that you can stand up under it" (1 Cor. 10:13).

Have you given thanks to God for the victory Christ has already won for you over the guilt and power of sin? Each day give thanks to God knowing that the "triumph of grace" is assured regardless of your struggle. "He who began a good work in you will carry it on to completion" (Phil. 1:6).

Part 9: Life in the Spirit

Romans 8:1–27

ROMANS 8:1–4

Therefore, there is now no condemnation for those who are in Christ Jesus, because through Christ Jesus the law of the Spirit of life set me free from the law of sin and death. For what the law was powerless to do in that it was weakened by the sinful nature, God did by sending his own Son in the likeness of sinful man to be a sin offering. And so he condemned sin in sinful man, in order that the righteous requirements of the law might be fully met in us, who do not live according to the sinful nature but according to the Spirit.

No Condemnation

Therefore, there is now no condemnation.

ROMANS 8:1

Each of the persons of the Godhead is involved in our salvation.

God the Father. What has God the Father done for our salvation? The answer is twofold. First, God sent Jesus in the likeness of sinful man to be a sin offering. Second, and by this means, God condemned sin in sinful man so that the righteous requirements of the law might be fully met in those who are joined to Christ.

God the Son. What has Jesus Christ done for our salvation? He became like us in order to become a sin offering. This has two parts. First, as a sin offering to God, Jesus made propitiation for our sins. Second, Jesus did a work of redemption.

God the Holy Spirit. What has the Holy Spirit done for our salvation? He has joined us to Christ, so that we become beneficiaries of all Christ has done. By joining us to Christ, the Holy Spirit seals our salvation and makes possible the great declaration of this chapter: "Therefore, there is now no condemnation for those who are in Christ Jesus."

89

A carpenter will sometimes join two boards by driving nails through them and then bending the protruding tip of the nails over sideways, embedding them in the wood, thus clinching the nail. Paul teaches that this is what the persons of the Godhead do for our eternal security. "There is now no condemnation" (1) because of the Father's work; (2) because of the Son's work; and (3) because of the work of the Holy Spirit. Now it is "no, nay, never" for those who are in Jesus.

But do not presume on this security. This is a great doctrine for those who truly are in Christ, but it is only for those who are in him. Make sure you are. If you are not sure, give the matter no rest until the Holy Spirit himself plants in your heart the assurance that you really are Christ's.

If you are not sure that you are in Christ, ask him now for the Holy Spirit to join you to him. Repent of your sins, call on Christ for salvation, and trust that you have been joined to him.

Those who live according to the sinful nature have their minds set on what that nature desires; but those who live in accordance with the Spirit have their minds set on what the Spirit desires. The mind of sinful man is death, but the mind controlled by the Spirit is life and peace; the sinful mind is hostile to God. It does not submit to God's law, nor can it do so. Those controlled by the sinful nature cannot please God.

You, however, are controlled not by the sinful nature but by the Spirit, if the Spirit of God lives in you. And if anyone does not have the Spirit of Christ, he does not belong to Christ. But if Christ is in you, your body is dead because of sin, yet your spirit is alive because of righteousness. And if the Spirit of him who raised Jesus from the dead is living in you, he who raised Christ from the dead will also give life to your mortal bodies through his Spirit, who lives in you.

Therefore, brothers, we have an obligation—but it is not to the sinful nature, to live according to it. For if you live according to the sinful nature, you will die; but if by the Spirit you put to death the misdeeds of the body, you will live, because those who are led by the Spirit of God are sons of God. For you did not receive a spirit that makes you a slave again to fear, but you received the Spirit of sonship. And by him we cry, "Abba, Father." The Spirit himself testifies with our spirit that we are God's children. Now if we are children, then we are heirs—heirs of God and co-heirs with Christ, if indeed we share in his sufferings in order that we may also share in his glory.

Sanctification: The Moral Imperative

Therefore, brothers, we have an obligation.
ROMANS 8:12

I once received a letter from an old friend that contained two questions: (1) How can I find the strength to do what is right; and (2) Why doesn't God intervene in my life in special ways to help out? My response went something like this.

I am sure you will find the strength to do what is right in this situation. The reason I know you have the strength you need is that you have the Holy Spirit, which is true of every Christian. And that is the answer to your other question too.

We often want to know why God does not intervene in our lives to do something special. But what do we mean when we ask that question? Do we mean we want God to reorder events to suit our own personal wishes? If so, we have no right to ask that, nor should we want to. That would mean we know better than God, that we can order the events of our lives better than he can. That would be terrible.

Or do we mean we want God to solve our problem by some external means, perhaps by removing the temptation, by changing our thinking so that we are no longer attracted by the wrong, or by providing an experience that will strip the temptation of its power? But if God were to do that, it would mean that what we are able to do as normal Christians unaided by some supernatural intervention of God does not count. What would be the point of being a Christian if, in crisis situations, God always has to intervene in some way.

To be a Christian means this. First, God has already done everything necessary to save you not only from sin's penalty but also from its power. You have God's Holy Spirit within you, and as a result, you can live for him.

Second, you will live for him. And not only will you live for him, putting to death the misdeeds of the body and living in accordance with the Holy Spirit's desires, but doing so will also matter profoundly. When Christians do the right thing—even when it breaks their hearts or when they suffer for it—and when they do it in utter dependence on God and out of love for him, then their obedience to God proves everything. It proves that they matter and that God matters. It proves that victory, their victory and yours, will endure to the praise of our great God throughout eternity.

Give thanks to God that he has given you his Spirit, who enables you to do the right thing, and that doing the right thing matters. Though no one else may seem to notice, your victory will endure to the praise of your great God throughout eternity.

I consider that our present sufferings are not worth comparing with the glory that will be revealed in us. The creation waits in eager expectation for the sons of God to be revealed. For the creation was subjected to frustration, not by its own choice, but by the will of the one who subjected it, in hope that the creation itself will be liberated from its bondage to decay and brought into the glorious freedom of the children of God.

We know that the whole creation has been groaning as in the pains of childbirth right up to the present time. Not only so, but we ourselves, who have the firstfruits of the Spirit, groan inwardly as we wait eagerly for our adoption as sons, the redemption of our bodies. For in this hope we were saved. But hope that is seen is no hope at all. Who hopes for what he already has? But if we hope for what we do not yet have, we wait for it patiently.

In the same way, the Spirit helps us in our weakness. We do not know what we ought to pray for, but the Spirit himself intercedes for us with groans that words cannot express. And he who searches our hearts knows the mind of the Spirit, because the Spirit intercedes for the saints in accordance with God's will.

The Incomparable Glory

I consider that our present sufferings are not worth comparing with the glory that will be revealed in us.

ROMANS 8:18

If we can appreciate what Paul is saying in this text and get it fixed in our minds, we will find it able to change the way we look at life and the way we live—more than anything else we can imagine. It will provide two things at least.

1. *Vision.* Focusing on the promise of glory will give us a vision of life in its eternal context, which means we will begin to see life here as it really is. We have two problems at this point. First, we are limited by our concept of time. We think in terms of the "threescore years and ten" allotted to us, or at best the few years that led up to our earthly existence or the few years after it. We do not have a long view. Second, we are limited by our materialism. Our reference point is what we perceive through our senses, so we have the greatest possible difficulty thinking of "the spirit" and other intangibles. We need to be delivered from this bondage and awakened from our spiritual blindness.

In "The Weight of Glory," C. S. Lewis addressed those who considered his talk about glory as only fantasy, the weaving of a spell. He replied by admitting that perhaps that is what he was trying to do. But he reminded his listeners that spells in fairy tales are of two kinds. Some induce enchantments. Others break them. "You and I have need of the strongest spell that can be found to wake us from the evil enchantment of worldliness which has been laid upon us for nearly a hundred years."[1]

2. *Endurance.* "Breaking the spell" will give us the strength to endure whatever hardships, temptations, persecutions, or physical suffering it pleases God to send us. Suppose there were no glory. Suppose this life really were all there is. If that were the case, I for one would not endure anything, at least nothing I could avoid. And I would probably break down under the tribulations I could not avoid. But knowing that an eternal glory awaits, I will try to do what pleases God and hang on in spite of anything.

Paul writes, "I consider that," meaning he has thought it through and concluded that "our present sufferings are not worth comparing with the glory that will be revealed in us" (Rom. 8:18). By using this phrase, he invites us to think it through also. If you are a Christian, I ask, "Isn't what the apostle says in this verse true? Isn't the glory to come worth anything you might be asked to face here, however painful or distressing?"

> *What is the hope that keeps you going? Is it a hope placed in things getting better in this life and world, or is it the gospel hope of the glory to come, the glory for which Christ saved you?*

Part 10: Unquenchable Love

Romans 8:28–39

ROMANS 8:28–30

And we know that in all things God works for the good of those who love him, who have been called according to his purpose. For those God foreknew he also predestined to be conformed to the likeness of his Son, that he might be the firstborn among many brothers. And those he predestined, he also called; those he called, he also justified; those he justified, he also glorified.

A Golden Chain of Five Links

*For those God foreknew he also predestined. . . . And
those he predestined, he also called; those he called,
he also justified; those he justified, he also glorified.*

ROMANS 8:29–30

When we are first saved we think naturally that we had a
great deal to do with it. But the longer we are a Christian,
the further we move from any feeling that we are responsible
for our salvation, or even any part of it, and the closer we
come to the conviction that it is all of God.

It is a good thing it is of God too! Because if it were accomplished by us, we could just as easily un-accomplish it—and
no doubt would. If God is the author, salvation is something
that is done wisely, well, and forever.

Robert Haldane provides this summary.

> In looking back on this passage, we should observe that, in all
> that is stated, man acts no part, but is passive, and all is done
> by God. He is elected and predestinated and called and justi-
> fied and glorified by God. The apostle was here concluding all
> that he had said before in enumerating topics of consolation
> to believers, and is now going on to show that God is "for
> us," or on the part of his people. Could anything, then, be
> more consolatory to those who love God, than to be in this

manner assured that the great concern of their salvation is not left in their own keeping?[1]

Years ago Harry A. Ironside, that great Bible teacher, told a story about an older Christian who was asked to give his testimony. The man told how God had sought him out and found him, how God had loved him, called him, saved him, delivered him, cleansed him, and healed him—a great witness to the grace, power, and glory of God. But after the meeting a rather legalistic brother took him aside and criticized his testimony, as certain of us like to do. He said, "I appreciated all you said about what God did for you. But you didn't mention anything about your part in it. Salvation is really part us and part God. You should have mentioned something about your part."

"Oh, yes," the older Christian said. "I apologize for that. I'm sorry. I really should have said something about my part. My part was running away, and his part was running after me until he caught me."[2]

We all have run away. But God has set his love on us, predestined us to become like Jesus Christ, called us to faith and repentance, justified us, yes, and even glorified us, so certain of completion is his plan. May he alone be praised!

Understanding that God does all that is involved in your salvation should lead you to two responses—to be comforted in the security of your salvation and to be moved to glorifying God alone. Take time to thank God for such comfort and to give him praise for running after you.

What, then, shall we say in response to this? If God is for us, who can be against us? He who did not spare his own Son, but gave him up for us all—how will he not also, along with him, graciously give us all things? Who will bring any charge against those whom God has chosen? It is God who justifies. Who is he that condemns? Christ Jesus, who died—more than that, who was raised to life—is at the right hand of God and is also interceding for us. Who shall separate us from the love of Christ? Shall trouble or hardship or persecution or famine or nakedness or danger or sword? As it is written:

> "For your sake we face death all day long;
> we are considered as sheep to be
> slaughtered."

No, in all these things we are more than conquerors through him who loved us. For I am convinced that neither death nor life, neither angels nor demons, neither the present nor the future, nor any powers, neither height nor depth, nor anything else in all creation, will be able to separate us from the love of God that is in Christ Jesus our Lord.

The Love of God in Christ Jesus

Nor anything else in all creation, will be able to separate us from the love of God that is in Christ Jesus our Lord.

ROMANS 8:39

What does "anything else in all creation" include? It includes everything that exists except God, since God created all these other things. Thus, if God is for us and if God controls everything else, since he made it, then absolutely nothing anywhere will be able to separate us from his love for us in Christ Jesus.

That reminds me of the word Paul uses in verse 38: *convinced*. This is Paul's personal testimony, but it is a testimony based on the soundest evidence, evidence that persuaded Paul and should persuade us also. What are the grounds of this persuasion? Paul's conviction is not based on the intensity of his feelings or a belief that the harsh circumstances of life are bound to improve or that any of these separating factors will somehow be dissolved or go away. Rather, it is based on the greatness of God's love for us in Christ, and that awesome love has been made known in that God sent his Son to die in our place.

There is nothing in all the universe greater or more steadfast than that love. *Therefore*, nothing in all the universe can separate us from it:

> not death, not life
> not angels, not demons
> not the present, not the future
> not any power
> not height, not depth
> not anything else in all creation

I do not know of anything greater than that. So I ask of you, Is this *your* testimony? Have you been persuaded of these truths, as Paul was? Can you say, "I no longer have any doubts. I know that salvation is entirely of God and that he will keep me safe until the very end"? If you are not certain of these truths, it is because you are still looking at yourself. You are thinking of your own feeble powers and not of God and his omnipotence.

As far as I am concerned, I am persuaded, and I am glad I am. There is nothing in all of heaven and earth to compare to this assurance.

Are you persuaded that nothing can separate you from the love of God that is in Christ Jesus? Rejoice that you are secure in his love, because that security rests entirely on God's promise made certain by Christ's redeeming work.

God and History

Chapters 9–11

Part 11: Paul and His People

Romans 9:1–5

ROMANS 9:1–5

I speak the truth in Christ—I am not lying, my conscience confirms it in the Holy Spirit—I have great sorrow and unceasing anguish in my heart. For I could wish that I myself were cursed and cut off from Christ for the sake of my brothers, those of my own race, the people of Israel. Theirs is the adoption as sons; theirs the divine glory, the covenants, the receiving of the law, the temple worship and the promises. Theirs are the patriarchs, and from them is traced the human ancestry of Christ, who is God over all, forever praised! Amen.

Great Sorrow for a Great People

I have great sorrow and unceasing anguish in my heart.

ROMANS 9:2

Let me ask you five thought-provoking questions:

1. *Do you anguish over others?* Do you sorrow for those who do not know Jesus Christ and who are therefore perishing without him? I am afraid most of us do not. Why is that? Is it because we do not believe they are perishing? Because we do not believe the gospel? Probably it is because we are not very much like Jesus Christ, do not spend much time with him, and do not think of spiritual things much at all.

2. *Do you anguish over those closest to you, the members of your own family?* Paul grieved for the Gentiles, but these verses deal with his own people and with his personal, special sorrow for them. If we were like him, husbands would grieve for unsaved wives, wives for unsaved husbands, parents for children, and children for parents. We would grieve for members of our extended families and for our neighborhoods.

3. *Do you anguish over those who are your enemies?* Paul's sorrow was also for those who were his avowed enemies. If you have enemies, you are to love them. In fact, you are to love most those who treat you worst. God loved us while we

were "enemies" (Rom. 5:10). How are we to win others unless we love even our enemies in this way?

4. *Do you anguish over those who are great sinners?* The nation for whom Paul grieved was composed of great sinners, for they had rejected the love of God in Christ Jesus. Do you similarly grieve for sinners? If you do not, is it because you do not really consider yourself one of them?

5. *Do you anguish over those who have great privileges?* Finally, the Jews of Paul's day possessed great privileges. So we are led to ask ourselves, "Do I anguish over those who are favored spiritually and in other ways, as well as over those who are openly sinners, downtrodden and unfortunate?" Those who are privileged need the gospel too.

I commend the heart of the great apostle to you. Let the sins of others grieve you. Let the fate that hangs over them like the sword of Damocles be often on your mind. If it is, you will work for their salvation in exactly the same proportion, and you will speak often of Jesus, who actually was accursed for those who should believe in him.

> *Do you anguish over the lost? Pray now by name for the salvation of members of your family and others God has placed in your life. Pray for God to grant you wisdom and courage to speak about Jesus to them.*

Part 12: The Justification of God

Romans 9:6–29

It is not as though God's word had failed. For not all who are descended from Israel are Israel. Nor because they are his descendants are they all Abraham's children. On the contrary, "It is through Isaac that your offspring will be reckoned." In other words, it is not the natural children who are God's children, but it is the children of the promise who are regarded as Abraham's offspring. For this was how the promise was stated: "At the appointed time I will return, and Sarah will have a son."

Not only that, but Rebekah's children had one and the same father, our father Isaac. Yet, before the twins were born or had done anything good or bad—in order that God's purpose in election might stand: not by works but by him who calls—she was told, "The older will serve the younger." Just as it is written: "Jacob I loved, but Esau I hated."

What then shall we say? Is God unjust? Not at all! For he says to Moses,

> "I will have mercy on whom I have mercy,
>   and I will have compassion on whom I have
>   compassion."

It does not, therefore, depend on man's desire or effort, but on God's mercy. For the Scripture says to Pharaoh: "I raised you up for this very purpose, that I might display my power in you and that my name might be proclaimed in all the earth." Therefore God has mercy on whom he wants to have mercy, and he hardens whom he wants to harden.

True Israel

For not all who are descended from Israel are Israel.

ROMANS 9:6

How can we be sure we are Christians? We need to answer a number of specific questions as we examine ourselves.

1. *Do I believe on Christ?* The first requirement is faith, because faith is our point of contact with the gospel. Ask yourself, "Have I believed on Jesus?" Not, "Have I believed on him in broad cultural terms?" but rather, "Have I been touched by the knowledge of Jesus's death for me, and have I committed myself to him? Am I serious about following after Christ, obeying his commands, and pleasing him?"

2. *Am I following after Christ?* The first question leads to the next: "Am I actually Jesus's follower?" Jesus called his followers with the words *follow me*. And when they followed him, their lives were inevitably redirected. Nobody who begins to follow Jesus Christ is ever entirely the same or walks in the same paths afterward. So ask yourself, "Has my life been redirected? Is there anything I am doing now that I did not do before or would not be doing were I not committed to Jesus? And are there things I have stopped doing? Is Jesus my very own Lord and Savior?"

3. *Do I testify to Christ?* This is a harder point for true self-examination, because it is easier for some to talk about Jesus than for others. Nevertheless, this is an important question and one worth asking. If you never speak to anyone about Jesus, how can you believe you really care about him and love him, not to mention care about and love the other person, who needs to receive the Savior?

4. *Am I learning about Christ?* "Am I trying to learn more and more about Jesus Christ? Do I know more about him today than I did at the time of my conversion? Or at this time last year?" How can you think of yourself as a Christian when you have no interest in learning about the one who gave himself for you?

Christian leaders say we need a revival. But what is a revival? A revival is the reviving of the alleged people of God, and it is preceded by an awakening in which many who thought themselves to be Christians come to their right senses and recognize that they are not new creatures in Christ and that all is not well with their souls. Revival begins in the church, not in the world. It begins with people like you. I, too, think we need a revival. But if it happens, why should it not begin with us? With you? May God grant it for his mercy's sake.

Take time now to examine yourself through these four questions. Pray for honesty before God for the sake of your soul.

One of you will say to me: "Then why does God still blame us? For who resists his will?" But who are you, O man, to talk back to God? "Shall what is formed say to him who formed it, 'Why did you make me like this?'" Does not the potter have the right to make out of the same lump of clay some pottery for noble purposes and some for common use?

What if God, choosing to show his wrath and make his power known, bore with great patience the objects of his wrath—prepared for destruction? What if he did this to make the riches of his glory known to the objects of his mercy, whom he prepared in advance for glory—even us, whom he also called, not only from the Jews but also from the Gentiles? As he says in Hosea:

> "I will call them 'my people' who are not my
>   people;
>   and I will call her 'my loved one' who is not
>   my loved one,"

and,

> "It will happen that in the very place where it
>   was said to them,
>   'You are not my people,'
> they will be called 'sons of the living God.'"

Isaiah cries out concerning Israel:

> "Though the number of the Israelites be like
>   the sand by the sea,
>   only the remnant will be saved.
> For the Lord will carry out
>   his sentence on earth with speed and
>   finality."

It is just as Isaiah said previously:

> "Unless the Lord Almighty
>   had left us descendants,
> we would have become like Sodom,
>   we would have been like Gomorrah."

The Patience of God

What if God, choosing to show his wrath and make his power known, bore with great patience the objects of his wrath—prepared for destruction?

ROMANS 9:22

Has the Lord's patience led you toward repentance? Is it doing so now? Let me help you think through the matter by these observations.

God is patient for a reason. If you are not in hell today, which you are not though you deserve to be, it is because God has been patient with you, and the purpose of his patience is to lead you to repentance. God's patience is a great thing. But you must not abuse it. It is meant to do you good. The day of God's patience is the day of his grace.

Think how patient God has been with you.

You have sinned against knowledge, and he has been exceedingly patient. You are not like the heathen, who know nothing of God or his salvation. You live in a country where the Scriptures are known, the doctrines of the Bible are taught, the way of salvation is proclaimed, and the path of godliness is held up for all to see. But you have spurned that knowledge.

You may also have sinned against grace, and still God has been patient. You may have been born into a Christian home, belong to a good church, have Christian friends who care for you, witness to you, and pray for you. But you have not profited from those gracious acts and circumstances.

You have even sinned against patience, and yet God has been exceedingly patient with you. You know that "love so amazing, so divine" demands your all. You have refused to give it, and still God has been patient with you.

God will not be patient forever. Although God's patience is great, it is not eternal. We are warned in Scripture that God's wrath has been withheld by his patience, but one day it will be poured forth. God's patience leads to repentance, but you must still repent. You must believe on Jesus. If you do not, you will face God's judgment in the end, however much you may scoff at it now.

Because God is patient, we should be patient. We tend to be impatient with other people, especially with those we are trying to win to Christ. But God is patient, and we should be also. It is not easy to be patient, but let us try to be. And the God who is himself patient may use our patience to draw many hurting people to the Savior.

> *If you have yet to make a decision for Christ, what is holding you back? How long will you test the patience of God? If you have turned to Christ, are you now exercising the same patience toward others? Are you patiently praying for the lost and witnessing to them?*

Part 13: Jewish Unbelief

Romans 9:30–10:21

What then shall we say? That the Gentiles, who did not pursue righteousness, have obtained it, a righteousness that is by faith; but Israel, who pursued a law of righteousness, has not attained it. Why not? Because they pursued it not by faith but as if it were by works. They stumbled over the "stumbling stone." As it is written:

> "See, I lay in Zion a stone that causes men to
>   stumble
>   and a rock that makes them fall,
> and the one who trusts in him will never be
>   put to shame."

Brothers, my heart's desire and prayer to God for the Israelites is that they may be saved. For I can testify about them that they are zealous for God, but their zeal is not based on knowledge. Since they did not know the righteousness that comes from God and sought to establish their own, they did not submit to God's righteousness. Christ is the end of the law so that there may be righteousness for everyone who believes.

Moses describes in this way the righteousness that is by the law: "The man who does these things will live by them." But the righteousness that is by faith says: "Do not say in your heart, 'Who will ascend into heaven?'" (that is, to bring Christ down) "or 'Who will descend into the deep?'" (that is, to bring Christ up from the dead). But what does it say? "The word is near you; it is in your mouth and in your heart," that is, the word of faith we are proclaiming: That if you confess with your mouth, "Jesus is Lord," and believe in your heart that God raised him from the dead, you will be saved. For it is with your heart that you believe and are justified, and it is with your mouth that you confess and are saved. As the Scripture says, "Anyone who trusts in him will never be put to shame." For there is no difference between Jew and Gentile—the same Lord is Lord of all and richly blesses all who call on him, for, "Everyone who calls on the name of the Lord will be saved."

Salvation for All

Everyone who calls on the name of the Lord will be saved.
ROMANS 10:13

The Bible's promise is that you will be saved if you believe on Jesus and trust in what he accomplished on the cross by dying for your sin. That is, you will be saved from your sin and from the wrath of God that hangs over you because of it.

I do not care what your condition up to this point has been. But don't put it off. You need to call on Jesus today. Consider the story of the SS *Edmund Fitzgerald*.

The *Edmund Fitzgerald* was a Great Lakes freighter nearly a thousand feet long. She had sailed to Duluth, Minnesota, to pick up iron ore, and now, during the first week of November 1975, she was making her way back across. The first day out, a terrible storm moved down out of Canada to the lakes. This was a particularly bad storm, with waves reaching twenty-five or thirty feet in height. The captain of a freighter that was following the *Edmund Fitzgerald*, from whom we have sworn testimony as to what happened, was worried.

Somewhere along the way, the *Edmund Fitzgerald* began to take on water and developed an increasingly strong list to starboard. She sank low in the water. The captain of the other ship kept in radio and radar contact, but the *Fitzgerald*'s captain kept reporting that everything was all right.

The last communication from the doomed freighter was this tragic message: "We are holding our own."

Minutes later the ship headed into a wave that washed over her low-lying decks, and she never came up. In less than ten seconds the *Edmund Fitzgerald* sank, with the loss of all twenty-nine people aboard. The captain of the other ship reported that she simply disappeared from his radar screen. One minute she was there. The next she was gone forever.

If you have not called on the Lord Jesus Christ for salvation, your state is like that of the stricken freighter. You are headed into judgment—and who can say how close you may be to the ultimate disaster?

Do not say, "I am holding my own." Only a fool would say that when he or she is sinking, and you are sinking. Instead, call on the name of the Lord Jesus Christ for salvation. Do so confidently, because, as our text says, "Everyone who calls on the name of the Lord will be saved."

Do not let pride or a false sense of security keep you from calling on the name of the Lord Jesus Christ for your salvation. Call on him now in faith to save you. If you have already called on Christ, give thanks to God for that great salvation.

How, then, can they call on the one they have not believed in? And how can they believe in the one of whom they have not heard? And how can they hear without someone preaching to them? And how can they preach unless they are sent? As it is written, "How beautiful are the feet of those who bring good news!"

But not all the Israelites accepted the good news. For Isaiah says, "Lord, who has believed our message?" Consequently, faith comes from hearing the message, and the message is heard through the word of Christ. But I ask: Did they not hear? Of course they did:

> "Their voice has gone out into all the earth,
>   their words to the ends of the world."

Again I ask: Did Israel not understand? First, Moses says,

> "I will make you envious by those who are not
>   a nation;
>   I will make you angry by a nation that has
>   no understanding."

And Isaiah boldly says,

> "I was found by those who did not seek me;
>   I revealed myself to those who did not ask
>   for me."

But concerning Israel he says,

> "All day long I have held out my hands
>   to a disobedient and obstinate people."

God's Beautiful People

As it is written, "How beautiful are the feet of those who bring good news!"

ROMANS 10:15

Do you know how the gospel came to Hugh Latimer (c. 1485–1555), that great bishop who became one of the brightest lights of the Protestant Reformation in England? Hugh Latimer was a "beautiful" man, strikingly good-looking and brilliant. But he did not know Christ, and he was using his learning to oppose the teachings of the Reformers, especially that of Philipp Melanchthon, Martin Luther's co-worker and friend.

Latimer was at Cambridge at this time and so was a little monk named Thomas Bilney. No one paid much attention to Bilney. But Bilney had discovered the gospel, and he wanted the great Hugh Latimer to come to Christ too. *What a tremendous influence he would have, if only he would discover the gospel of God's grace in Christ*, Bilney thought.

So he hit on a plan. One day after Latimer finished preaching, Bilney caught his arm as he was coming out of the church and asked if he would hear his confession. That was a prescribed duty of a priest. So Latimer listened to Bilney, and the monk who had found Christ "confessed" the gospel, sharing

how it had changed his life. Latimer later said he was converted by Bilney's gospel "confession." As for Latimer, he
became a great reformer in England and is best known for
his encouragement of Nicholas Ridley as they were being led
to the stake at the height of the English persecutions in 1555:
"Be of good comfort, Master Ridley, and play the man; we
shall this day light such a candle by God's grace in England
as [I trust] shall never be put out."

Bilney was not a beautiful person as we generally think of
beauty. But he was the bearer of the gospel to Hugh Latimer,
and that means he was beautiful in the sight of God, as are
all those who obey the Lord Jesus Christ in carrying out the
Great Commission.

May I suggest you start thinking of beauty the way God
does. What you think is beautiful now is going to be a thing
of the past in just a few short years. Those you think beautiful now will no longer be beautiful in physical terms. But the
beauty of the bearers of the gospel will last forever. What
is more, they will go on getting more and more beautiful as
they use not only this life but also eternity to praise the Lord
Jesus Christ more fully.

Beauty really is as beauty does. I invite you to value others not by their outward appearance but by their service to
Jesus Christ and the gospel. And I invite you to become one
of God's beautiful people yourself.

*Isn't it a wonderful comfort to know that the true beauty God
values is the service rendered to Jesus Christ and the gospel? In
what ways are you serving now? Pray for God to make you aware
of opportunities—great and small—to render service.*

Part 14: The Times of the Gentiles

Romans 11:1–32

I ask then: Did God reject his people? By no means! I am an Israelite myself, a descendant of Abraham, from the tribe of Benjamin. God did not reject his people, whom he foreknew. Don't you know what the Scripture says in the passage about Elijah—how he appealed to God against Israel: "Lord, they have killed your prophets and torn down your altars; I am the only one left, and they are trying to kill me"? And what was God's answer to him? "I have reserved for myself seven thousand who have not bowed the knee to Baal." So too, at the present time there is a remnant chosen by grace. And if by grace, then it is no longer by works; if it were, grace would no longer be grace.

What then? What Israel sought so earnestly it did not obtain, but the elect did. The others were hardened, as it is written:

> "God gave them a spirit of stupor,
> eyes so that they could not see
> and ears so that they could not hear,
> to this very day."

And David says:

> "May their table become a snare and a trap,
> a stumbling block and a retribution for
> them.
> May their eyes be darkened so they cannot see,
> and their backs be bent forever."

Again I ask: Did they stumble so as to fall beyond recovery? Not at all! Rather, because of their transgression, salvation has come to the Gentiles to make Israel envious. But if their transgression means riches for the world, and their loss means riches for the Gentiles, how much greater riches will their fullness bring!

I am talking to you Gentiles. Inasmuch as I am the apostle to the Gentiles, I make much of my ministry in the hope that I may somehow arouse my own people to envy and save some of them. For if their rejection is the reconciliation of the world, what will their acceptance be but life from the dead? If the part of the dough offered as firstfruits is holy, then the whole batch is holy; if the root is holy, so are the branches.

If some of the branches have been broken off, and you, though a wild olive shoot, have been grafted in among the others and now share in the nourishing sap from the olive root, do not boast over those branches. If you do, consider this: You do not support the root, but the root supports you. You will say then, "Branches were broken off so that I could be grafted in." Granted. But they were broken off because of unbelief, and you stand by faith. Do not be arrogant, but be afraid. For if God did not spare the natural branches, he will not spare you either.

Holy to the Lord

If the part of the dough offered as first-
fruits is holy, then the whole batch is holy;
if the root is holy, so are the branches.

ROMANS 11:16

Our destiny as Christians is the same as that of the nation of Israel. We, too, are to be holy to the Lord. And if that is the case, if that is what we will surely be one day—since "without holiness no one will see the Lord" (Heb. 12:14)—we must strive to be holy now.

Have you ever thought of your destiny in terms of holiness? If you are a Christian, you have been set apart for God to be wholly his. But you are not holy now. You are sinful now, and the more you live, the more you will be aware of it. Your *destiny* is holiness. That is why we read about this so often in the Bible. God told the people through Moses, "Be holy, because I am holy" (Lev. 11:44; cf. 19:2; 20:7). And Peter picks up on the theme, writing, "But just as he who called you is holy, so be holy in all you do; for it is written: 'Be holy, because I am holy'" (1 Peter 1:15–16). This is not only a command. It is our sure end. If we belong to Jesus Christ, God, whose purposes do not change, will make us like him in holiness one day.

We usually think of salvation relationally today. That is why we think of God's attributes as being, first of all, love, then perhaps mercy, kindness, goodness, and such things. This is not wrong, of course. God is love, and we are enabled to love him and others because he first loved us and therefore showed us what love is like.

But this is not the way the Bible speaks of our destiny. It is not the love relationship that is emphasized. We are not told we will spend our time in heaven loving God and others, though we undoubtedly will. The Bible emphasizes holiness. And the reason it does is that a lack of holiness is what accounts for our inability to love rightly and, in fact, to do anything else well. The reason our relationships with God are not all they should be is that we are not holy. The reason our relationships with others are not all they should be is that we are not holy. We need to be holy.

But, praise God, one day we will be holy. "We shall be like him [Jesus], for we shall see him as he is" (1 John 3:2).

So why not be holy now? That is what John concludes, for immediately after telling us that we will be like Jesus one day, he says, "Everyone who has this hope in him purifies himself, just as he is pure" (v. 3). Do you? You will, if you have your eyes fixed on that great destiny.

How seriously do you take being holy to the Lord? Perhaps troubles you have in relationships are due to a greater desire for personal fulfillment and happiness than for holiness.

131

Consider therefore the kindness and sternness of God: sternness to those who fell, but kindness to you, provided that you continue in his kindness. Otherwise, you also will be cut off. And if they do not persist in unbelief, they will be grafted in, for God is able to graft them in again. After all, if you were cut out of an olive tree that is wild by nature, and contrary to nature were grafted into a cultivated olive tree, how much more readily will these, the natural branches, be grafted into their own olive tree!

I do not want you to be ignorant of this mystery, brothers, so that you may not be conceited: Israel has experienced a hardening in part until the full number of the Gentiles has come in. And so all Israel will be saved, as it is written:

> "The deliverer will come from Zion;
>   he will turn godlessness away from Jacob.
> And this is my covenant with them
>   when I take away their sins."

As far as the gospel is concerned, they are enemies on your account; but as far as election is concerned, they are loved on account of the patriarchs, for God's gifts and his call are irrevocable. Just as you who were at one time disobedient to God have now received mercy as a result of their disobedience, so they too have now become disobedient in order that they too may now receive mercy as a result of God's mercy to you. For God has bound all men over to disobedience so that he may have mercy on them all.

The Mystery of Jewish Hardening

*I do not want you to be ignorant of this mystery,
brothers, so that you may not be conceited.*

ROMANS 11:25

Here are two lessons to learn.

1. *We should not be conceited in thinking that in ourselves
we are something special.*

We have the tendency to assume that the reason we are
saved and others are not saved is because we are wiser or
more holy or more perceptive or more significant than they
are. We are not saved for any of these reasons. On the contrary, "God chose the foolish things of the world to shame
the wise; God chose the weak things of the world to shame
the strong. He chose the lowly things of this world and the
despised things—and the things that are not—to nullify the
things that are, so that no one may boast before him" (1 Cor.
1:27–29).

If God has chosen the foolish things now and will one
day renew a work among his ancient people when the times
of the Gentiles have been completed, we can never suppose
that we are special. Instead, we can only acknowledge that
we are saved on account of the mercy of God and by his
immeasurable grace.

2. We should not be conceited in thinking that other people, who are not like us, are hopeless.

It is easy for us to abandon hope for others. When we see a person who has squandered his or her spiritual opportunities or who has vigorously opposed Christianity or has sinned in some particularly dreadful fashion, we conclude that there is probably no chance for such a person. We write him or her off. But we must not think that way, for it is never true. God is the God of all hopeless causes, ourselves included. John Newton was surely close to God's heart when he replied to someone who spoke of an acquaintance for whom he despaired, "I have never despaired of any man since God saved me."

What about you? You may be laboring under the thought that you are a hopeless case, because of who you are or because of something you have done or said or thought. Or you may have a family member whose case seems hopeless. I assure you on the basis of the Word of God that the case is not hopeless. And you are not hopeless either! Only unbelief keeps a person from salvation, and even today you may still call on the name of the Lord and be wonderfully saved.

Are you guilty of thinking God has saved you because of something special he saw in you? Have you given up on someone else receiving salvation? Confess your lack of faith and pray for that individual now.

Part 15: Doxology

Romans 11:33–36

Oh, the depth of the riches of the wisdom and
  knowledge of God!
How unsearchable his judgments,
  and his paths beyond tracing out!
"Who has known the mind of the Lord?
  Or who has been his counselor?"
"Who has ever given to God,
  that God should repay him?"
For from him and through him and to him are
  all things.
  To him be the glory forever! Amen.

Soli Deo Gloria

To him be the glory forever! Amen.
ROMANS 11:36

Romans 11:36 is the first doxology in the letter. It is followed by another at the end, which is like it, though more complete: "To the only wise God be glory forever through Jesus Christ! Amen" (Rom. 16:27). It is significant that both doxologies speak of the glory of God and of forever. Two questions help us understand them.

1. *Who is to be glorified?* The answer is the sovereign God. For the most part, we start with man and man's needs. But Paul always started with God, and he ended with him too.

2. *Why should God be glorified?* The answer is that "from him and through him and to him are all things," particularly the work of salvation. Why is man saved? It is not because of anything in men and women themselves but because of God's grace. God elected us to it. God predestinated his elect people to salvation from before the foundation of the world. How is man saved? The answer is by the redeeming work of the Lord Jesus, the very Son of God. We could not save ourselves, but God saved us through the vicarious, atoning death of Jesus Christ. By what power are we brought to faith in Jesus? The answer is by the power of the Holy Spirit through what theo-

logians call effectual calling. God's call quickens us to new life. How can we become holy? Holiness is not something that originates in us, is achieved by us, or is sustained by us. It is due to God's joining us to Jesus so that we become different persons than we were before he did it. We have died to sin and been made alive to righteousness. Now there is no direction for us to go in the Christian life but forward. Where are we headed? To heaven, because Jesus is preparing a place in heaven for us. How can we be sure of arriving there? Because God, who began the work of our salvation, will continue it until we do. God never begins a work that he does not eventually bring to a happy and complete conclusion.

"To him be the glory forever! Amen."

So let us give God the glory, remembering that God himself says:

> I am the LORD; that is my name!
> I will not give my glory to another
> or my praise to idols (Isa. 42:8).

and

> For my own sake, for my own sake, I do this.
> How can I let myself be defamed?
> I will not yield my glory to another (Isa. 48:11).

Take time now to lift up your own doxology to God. Give glory to your Creator, your Redeemer, and your Sustainer.

SECTION 4

The New Humanity

Chapters 12–16

Part 16: Applied Christianity

Romans 12:1–2

ROMANS 12:1-2

Therefore, I urge you, brothers, in view of God's mercy, to offer your bodies as living sacrifices, holy and pleasing to God—this is your spiritual act of worship. Do not conform any longer to the pattern of this world, but be transformed by the renewing of your mind. Then you will be able to test and approve what God's will is—his good, pleasing and perfect will.

The Pattern of This Age

*Do not conform any longer to the pattern of this world,
but be transformed by the renewing of your mind.*

ROMANS 12:2

Note what Paul says we are to be: not *conformed* but *transformed* by the renewing of our minds. There is a deliberate distinction between those two words. Conformity is something that happens to you outwardly. Transformation happens inwardly. The Greek word translated "transformed" is *metamorphoô*, from which we get *metamorphosis*. It is what happens to a lowly caterpillar when it turns into a beautiful butterfly.

This Greek word is found four times in the New Testament: once here, once in 2 Corinthians 3:18 to describe our being transformed into the glorious likeness of Jesus Christ, and twice in the Gospels regarding the transfiguration of Jesus on the mountain where he had gone with Peter, James, and John. Those verses say, "There he was transfigured before them" (Matt. 17:2; Mark 9:2). The same word Paul uses to describe our transformation by the renewing of our minds so that we will not be conformed to this world is used by the Gospel writers to describe the transfiguration of Jesus from the form of his earthly humiliation to the radiance that Peter, James, and John were privileged to witness for a time.

And that is why Paul writes as he does in 2 Corinthians, saying, "We, who with unveiled faces all reflect the Lord's glory, are being transformed into his likeness with ever-increasing glory, which comes from the Lord, who is the Spirit" (3:18).

In 2 Corinthians Paul says, "It is happening." In Romans 12 he says, "Let it happen," thus putting the responsibility, though not the power to accomplish this necessary transformation, on us. How does it happen? Through the renewing of our minds, and the way our minds become renewed is by study of the life-giving and renewing Word of God. Without that study we remain in the world's mold, unable to think and therefore also unable to act as Christians. With that study, blessed and empowered as it will be by the Holy Spirit, we begin to take on something of the glorious luster of the Lord Jesus Christ and become increasingly like him.

> If transformation takes place through the renewal of your mind, what then are you doing to renew yours? Determine now to be a lifelong student of God's Word. Study it. Read books that help you understand it better. Listen to sermons and teachings that carefully explain it.

Part 17: The Christian and Other People

Romans 12:3–21

For by the grace given me I say to every one of you: Do not think of yourself more highly than you ought, but rather think of yourself with sober judgment, in accordance with the measure of faith God has given you. Just as each of us has one body with many members, and these members do not all have the same function, so in Christ we who are many form one body, and each member belongs to all the others. We have different gifts, according to the grace given us. If a man's gift is prophesying, let him use it in proportion to his faith. If it is serving, let him serve; if it is teaching, let him teach; if it is encouraging, let him encourage; if it is contributing to the needs of others, let him give generously; if it is leadership, let him govern diligently; if it is showing mercy, let him do it cheerfully.

Love must be sincere. Hate what is evil; cling to what is good. Be devoted to one another in brotherly love. Honor one another above yourselves. Never be lacking in zeal, but keep your spiritual fervor, serving the Lord. Be joyful in hope, patient in affliction, faithful in prayer. Share with God's people who are in need. Practice hospitality.

One Body in Christ

So in Christ we who are many form one body,
and each member belongs to all the others.

ROMANS 12:5

What is the challenge to informed biblical Christians in an individualistic age like ours? The answer is not the ecumenical movement. Our task is not to create the unity of the body, above all, not from the top down. The unity of the body is a given for those who are "in Christ." Nevertheless, we should work for any valid visible expression of our oneness in Christ that is attainable, and we should avoid unnecessary divisions and even try to learn from one another in a humble, teachable spirit.

Donald Grey Barnhouse tells how he once made slighting remarks about a denomination he considered to be on the fringe of genuine Christianity. A minister from this denomination was present and afterward told Barnhouse how grieved he was at what he considered an unjust judgment. Barnhouse apologized and suggested meeting for lunch with four or five ministers from this particular church.

When they got together, Barnhouse made the suggestion that during lunch they should discuss only the points on which they agreed. Afterward, when they had finished, they

147

could talk about their differences. They began to talk about Jesus Christ and what he meant to each of them. The tension abated, and there was a measure of joy as each confessed that Jesus was born of a virgin, that he came to die for our sins, and that he rose again bodily. Each acknowledged Jesus Christ as Lord. Each agreed that Jesus was now in heaven at the right hand of God the Father praying for his church. They confessed that he had sent his Holy Spirit at Pentecost and that the Lord was living in each of his children by means of the Holy Spirit. They acknowledged the reality of the new birth and that they were looking forward to the return of Jesus Christ, after which they would be spending eternity together.

By this time the meal was drawing to a close. When they turned to the matters that divided them, they found that they were indeed secondary—not unimportant but secondary. They recognized that they could agree to disagree about these matters without denying that each was nevertheless a member of Christ's body. Barnhouse confessed, "Though separated by a continent, I have often prayed for these men and am confident that they have prayed for me. We know that we are one in Christ. They made a distinct contribution to my spiritual life, and I contributed to theirs. I am the richer since I became acquainted with them."[1] Something like that would be a very good experience for most of us.

Are you quick to point out the differences of other professing Christians? Pray now for blessings on individuals different from you but who nevertheless proclaim Christ as Lord.

Bless those who persecute you; bless and do not curse. Rejoice with those who rejoice; mourn with those who mourn. Live in harmony with one another. Do not be proud, but be willing to associate with people of low position. Do not be conceited.

Do not repay anyone evil for evil. Be careful to do what is right in the eyes of everybody. If it is possible, as far as it depends on you, live at peace with everyone. Do not take revenge, my friends, but leave room for God's wrath, for it is written: "It is mine to avenge; I will repay," says the Lord. On the contrary:

> "If your enemy is hungry, feed him;
>   if he is thirsty, give him something to drink.
> In doing this, you will heap burning coals on
>   his head."

Do not be overcome by evil, but overcome evil with good.

The Christian and His Enemies

Live in harmony with one another.

ROMANS 12:16

Paul is thinking of how Christians should relate to unbelievers. Such a relationship includes the following.

Empathy. Empathy describes what Paul is talking about when he says, "Rejoice with those who rejoice; mourn with those who mourn" (Rom. 12:15). Empathy is the ability to identify closely with someone else, to make his case your own and allow what has happened to him to affect you also.

Amicability. Christians should be easy to get along with. This is what Paul is thinking of in verse 16 when he says we should "live in harmony with one another." He is talking about not making sparks or causing turmoil. If he is speaking in regard to our enemies, which is the case since the verses both before and after speak of them, then he is saying we should not be like those Christian crusaders who are always looking for a fight or hunting down "Christ's enemies." We are to love and win people, not root them out to beat them senseless.

The common touch. Christians should "be willing to associate with people of low position" (Rom. 12:16) even more than others, because that is what most of us are. We are to associate with those who seem unimportant even if we have a high position. We need to stop thinking of other people as being beneath us and instead regard them as people made for everlasting fellowship with God.

Humility. The sentence above takes us back to where Paul began. He said in verse 3, "Do not think of yourself more highly than you ought, but rather think of yourself with sober judgment." Can we do it? Leon Morris makes a helpful suggestion when he reminds us that "the person who is wise in his own eyes is rarely so in the eyes of other people."[1]

The trouble with exhortations of this nature, practical as they may be, is that they seem far beyond us and therefore discourage us if we take them seriously. If we examine ourselves, we will have to admit that we do not often pray for God's blessing on our enemies, empathize with others, act agreeably, associate with those the world scorns, or act in a humble manner. And that is discouraging. Perhaps what we need to do here is simply get our minds off ourselves entirely and think of Christ, because if we think of him, we will become increasingly like him.

> Think of a person who causes you grief. Think now of the love Christ has shown to you as a sinner. Can you pray for this person as Christ prays for you?

Part 18: Church and State

Romans 13:1–7

Everyone must submit himself to the governing authorities, for there is no authority except that which God has established. The authorities that exist have been established by God. Consequently, he who rebels against the authority is rebelling against what God has instituted, and those who do so will bring judgment on themselves. For rulers hold no terror for those who do right, but for those who do wrong. Do you want to be free from fear of the one in authority? Then do what is right and he will commend you. For he is God's servant to do you good. But if you do wrong, be afraid, for he does not bear the sword for nothing. He is God's servant, an agent of wrath to bring punishment on the wrongdoer. Therefore, it is necessary to submit to the authorities, not only because of possible punishment but also because of conscience.

This is also why you pay taxes, for the authorities are God's servants, who give their full time to governing. Give everyone what you owe him: If you owe taxes, pay taxes; if revenue, then revenue; if respect, then respect; if honor, then honor.

To Each His Due

Give everyone what you owe him.
ROMANS 13:7

How do we honor God? We do it by studying his Word that we may come to know him. When we discover something in his Word that he requires of us, we honor him by doing what he has commanded. We honor him by thanking him for all he has given and by praising him for all he is in and of himself. We honor God by trusting him through the many trials and disappointments of life. We honor him by praising him as the source of whatever good may be found in us or whatever good we may do in this life.

In a wonderful scene in Revelation 4:10–11, the saints stand before God represented by the twenty-four elders. They lay their crowns before the throne and say:

> You are worthy, our Lord and God,
>   to receive glory and honor and power,
> for you created all things,
>   and by your will they were created
>   and have their being.

It is the elders' way of showing that anything they accomplished was accomplished by the grace of God and by him only. So they give their crowns to God and praise him.

It is only as Christians capture the high ground of doing what they do for the honor and glory of God that they can be used by God to elevate society to where those who deserve honor are given honor and those who deserve respect are given respect. And it is only when that happens that a nation becomes morally strong and justice becomes a reality and not just a hollow word. In other words, a nation does not become strong by laws but by the character of its citizens.

The wonderful thing is that if we begin showing respect to those to whom respect is due and honor to those to whom honor is due, above all showing honor and respect to God, then others may learn something of God through us and eventually come to respect, honor, and love him too, which is salvation and the beginning of wisdom. "To each his due" is not only a word about taxes. It is about justice too and about the foundation of a free and just society.

Do you give due respect to those in authority over you, especially to those with whom you disagree? You can capture this high ground if your primary motive in life is to honor and glorify God.

Part 19: The Law of Love

Romans 13:8–14

Let no debt remain outstanding, except the continuing debt to love one another, for he who loves his fellowman has fulfilled the law. The commandments, "Do not commit adultery," "Do not murder," "Do not steal," "Do not covet," and whatever other commandment there may be, are summed up in this one rule: "Love your neighbor as yourself." Love does no harm to its neighbor. Therefore love is the fulfillment of the law.

And do this, understanding the present time. The hour has come for you to wake up from your slumber, because our salvation is nearer now than when we first believed. The night is nearly over; the day is almost here. So let us put aside the deeds of darkness and put on the armor of light. Let us behave decently, as in the daytime, not in orgies and drunkenness, not in sexual immorality and debauchery, not in dissension and jealousy. Rather, clothe yourselves with the Lord Jesus Christ, and do not think about how to gratify the desires of the sinful nature.

The Debt of Love

Let no debt remain outstanding, except the continuing debt to love one another, for he who loves his fellowman has fulfilled the law.

ROMANS 13:8

In addition to refraining from doing harm to our neighbor, real love also involves positive action. It "does" for the other. This is what Paul means when he writes of the "continuing debt to love one another."

Let's think about this "continuing debt" positively and ask, "What does it mean to discharge this debt honestly?" Here are some extremely simple but important and often neglected ways.

Listen to one another. We live in an age in which few people really listen to one another. We talk to or at one another, of course. To really love another person we must listen. If we do not know how to listen, we must learn how. And we must take time to do it.

Share with one another. The second thing we need to do is share ourselves with others. The problem is that sharing ourselves makes us vulnerable, especially if we are trying to share with a person we care deeply about. We are afraid to be vulnerable. Sharing is the reverse side of listening. We listen to the other person as he or she shares. Then we share ourselves. This is the only way to show real love and build real relationships.

Forgive one another. None of us is without sin. Therefore, we are all guilty of sinning against others. For this reason, listening and sharing also involve forgiveness. Sharing means expressing our hurts, and listening means hearing how we have hurt the other person.

Serve one another. The fourth practical expression of what it means to love one another is service. This does not come to us naturally, which is one reason the Bible mentions and illustrates it so often. This was practically the last lesson Jesus left with the disciples when he washed their feet. Jesus provided an example of menial service, teaching that we are to serve others.

What the world needs is the sincere, selfless, sacrificial, serving love of God displayed in those who know him and are determined to obey him faithfully. If you know Jesus, you will not follow after the world's selfish ways but instead will love as God loves. You will keep the law: "Love is the fulfillment of the law" (Rom. 13:10). But you will also go out of your way to listen to, share with, forgive, and serve other people.

Take these four ways of loving and examine how well you are doing in loving your neighbor. Pray for a specific "neighbor," asking God to use you to show his love to this individual.

160

Part 20: Christian Liberty

Romans 14:1–15:13

Accept him whose faith is weak, without passing judgment on disputable matters. One man's faith allows him to eat everything, but another man, whose faith is weak, eats only vegetables. The man who eats everything must not look down on him who does not, and the man who does not eat everything must not condemn the man who does, for God has accepted him. Who are you to judge someone else's servant? To his own master he stands or falls. And he will stand, for the Lord is able to make him stand.

One man considers one day more sacred than another; another man considers every day alike. Each one should be fully convinced in his own mind. He who regards one day as special, does so to the Lord. He who eats meat, eats to the Lord, for he gives thanks to God; and he who abstains, does so to the Lord and gives thanks to God. For none of us lives to himself alone and none of us dies to himself alone. If we live, we live to the Lord; and if we die, we die to the Lord. So, whether we live or die, we belong to the Lord.

For this very reason, Christ died and returned to life so that he might be the Lord of both the dead and the living. You, then, why do you judge your brother? Or why do you look down on your brother? For we will all stand before God's judgment seat. It is written:

> "'As surely as I live,' says the Lord,
> 'every knee will bow before me;
>   every tongue will confess to God.'"

So then, each of us will give an account of himself to God.

Therefore let us stop passing judgment on one another. Instead, make up your mind not to put any stumbling block or obstacle in your brother's way. As one who is in the Lord Jesus, I am fully convinced that no food is unclean in itself. But if anyone regards something as unclean, then for him it is unclean. If your brother is distressed because of what you eat, you are no longer acting in love. Do not by your eating destroy your brother for whom Christ died. Do not allow what you consider good to be spoken of as evil. For the kingdom of God is not a matter of eating and drinking, but of righteousness, peace and joy in the Holy Spirit, because anyone who serves Christ in this way is pleasing to God and approved by men.

Where Is the Chasm?

*Accept him whose faith is weak, without pass-
ing judgment on disputable matters.*

ROMANS 14:1

Let's allow God to deal with each of his servants how, when,
and as kindly as he will. And while we are at it, let's be thankful that he has dealt as kindly as he has with us. If he had
not, we would all be in deep trouble.

Take notice here that Paul has two initial points of advice.
In fact, what he says is stronger than advice—these are commands, and the whole sentence is made up of them: "Accept
him whose faith is weak" and "Do not pass judgment on
disputable matters."

Accept him whose faith is weak. This means we are to accept other Christians as Christians, and, as John Murray says,
"There is to be no discrimination in respect of confidence,
esteem, and affection."[1]

Accept is a strong term, because it is used of God's acceptance of us in verse 3 and of Christ's acceptance of us in
15:7. Verse 3 says, "The man who does not eat everything
must not condemn the man who does, for God has accepted
him." The other verse says, "Accept one another, then, just as

Christ accepted you." If God has accepted the other person, who are you not to accept him?

Do not pass judgment on disputable matters. Recognize that some standards of right conduct are unclear and that other matters really do not matter. In those areas let the matter drop and get on with things that do matter. Above all, accept the other believer for what he or she has to offer the whole body of Christ. And do your own part too! Tell someone about Jesus. Certainly you have better things to do than to hunt out the speck in the eye of your fellow Christian while overlooking the plank in your own.

Francis Schaeffer used to talk about "the chasm." He said we put it in the wrong place, dividing ourselves from other Christians. It shouldn't be there. True, there is a chasm between those who know Jesus Christ and those who do not, between Christians and the world, and it is a deep one. But that is where it lies, between Christians and the world, not between Christians and Christians. All who know Jesus Christ are on this side of the chasm, and we must stand with them for Christ's kingdom.

> *It is a critical matter to examine ourselves. Do we allow secondary matters to divide us from other believers, keeping us from working and worshiping together? Pray, asking God to forgive and change our judgmental attitudes.*

Let us therefore make every effort to do what leads to peace and to mutual edification. Do not destroy the work of God for the sake of food. All food is clean, but it is wrong for a man to eat anything that causes someone else to stumble. It is better not to eat meat or drink wine or to do anything else that will cause your brother to fall.

So whatever you believe about these things keep between yourself and God. Blessed is the man who does not condemn himself by what he approves. But the man who has doubts is condemned if he eats, because his eating is not from faith; and everything that does not come from faith is sin.

We who are strong ought to bear with the failings of the weak and not to please ourselves. Each of us should please his neighbor for his good, to build him up. For even Christ did not please himself but, as it is written: "The insults of those who insult you have fallen on me." For everything that was written in the past was written to teach us, so that through endurance and the encouragement of the Scriptures we might have hope.

Building Up or Tearing Down

Each of us should please his neigh-
bor for his good, to build him up.

ROMANS 15:2

Is all this worth it? Is it worthwhile to sharpen our skills and develop our Christian character so that others might grow to be like Jesus Christ? Of course it is. The problem is not that we doubt the ultimate value of the work we are given to do but that we get bogged down in the hard, daily task of fashioning the stones of this building and fitting them to the overall structure. We take our eyes off the blueprint and get bogged down in the rubble.

It helps to remember that what God is building is a temple. Here is an illustration. We are told in 1 Kings 6:7 that when the great temple of Solomon was constructed "only blocks dressed at the quarry were used, and no hammer, chisel or any other iron tool was heard at the temple site while it was being built." To my knowledge, no other building in history was ever built in this way. Its construction was so well done that it was almost silent. Silently, silently the stones were added, and the building rose.

So it is with the church. We do not hear what is going on inside human hearts as the Holy Spirit creates new life and adds individuals to the temple he is building. We do not even fully realize the part we are playing as we seek to build up these other people by focusing on the important matters, laying aside petty differences, and teaching the Word of God to them faithfully. But God is working, and the temple is rising. In the days of the apostles God was adding Gentiles to his church. Paul was his chief instrument in carrying the gospel to them. God added the high and low, slaves and freemen, Greeks, Romans, and barbarians. He added many at the time of the Reformation and in the days of the Great Awakenings and revivals.

He is still building his church today, and we are his workmen, laborers together with Jesus Christ. We have a responsibility to do the work well.

Do you realize that your individual acts of building up your fellow Christians are helping to build the temple of God, his church? Pray that the Lord will use you today. It may be through an act of service, a spoken word, or a prayer.

May the God who gives endurance and encouragement give you a spirit of unity among yourselves as you follow Christ Jesus, so that with one heart and mouth you may glorify the God and Father of our Lord Jesus Christ.

Accept one another, then, just as Christ accepted you, in order to bring praise to God. For I tell you that Christ has become a servant of the Jews on behalf of God's truth, to confirm the promises made to the patriarchs so that the Gentiles may glorify God for his mercy, as it is written:

> "Therefore I will praise you among the
>   Gentiles;
>   I will sing hymns to your name."

Again, it says,

> "Rejoice, O Gentiles, with his people."

And again,

> "Praise the Lord, all you Gentiles,
>   and sing praises to him, all you peoples."

And again, Isaiah says,

> "The Root of Jesse will spring up,
>   one who will arise to rule over the nations;
>   the Gentiles will hope in him."

May the God of hope fill you with all joy and peace as you trust in him, so that you may overflow with hope by the power of the Holy Spirit.

A Prayer for Unity

*So that with one heart and mouth you may glorify
the God and Father of our Lord Jesus Christ.*

ROMANS 15:6

Consider this important purpose clause: "*so that* with one heart and mouth you may glorify the God and Father of our Lord Jesus Christ."

According to this verse, the purpose of our unity is not so that the church might be a pleasant place to be or that weak Christians might be encouraged and strong Christians might be channeled into useful work. Rather, it is that God might be glorified. God must be made known as the great and wonderful God he is. Moreover, that is to take place as Christians with *one heart* (that is, in unity) praise him before others *with their mouths.*

From time to time I get letters from or speak to people who say they have trouble with the multiplicity of Christian denominations. In fact, I have a letter on my desk that says this even as I write this paragraph. Their argument is that denominations reflect negatively on the church and weaken its witness.

I am not sure that is the case or even that this is what really concerns these people. No one criticizes capitalism because there are many competing corporations, or the automobile industry because there is fierce rivalry among the automakers or between American companies and their Japanese or European counterparts.

I don't think the world is even particularly troubled by the fact that Christians disagree on some doctrinal matters. After all, they disagree with other people too.

The real problem is that Christians often do not appreciate and support one another, recognizing that whatever differences may exist, all who are Christ's followers nevertheless belong to the same family, fellowship, and body and therefore belong to one another. That is how, above all other ways, the God and Father of our Lord Jesus Christ must be glorified by us before the watching world.

Pray for Christians and churches with practices different from yours. Thank God for the ministry he is doing through them. Pray that he will receive glory from both them and you as you both seek to exalt the Lord Jesus Christ.

Part 21: Paul's Personal Ministry and Plans

Romans 15:14–33

I myself am convinced, my brothers, that you yourselves are full of goodness, complete in knowledge and competent to instruct one another. I have written you quite boldly on some points, as if to remind you of them again, because of the grace God gave me to be a minister of Christ Jesus to the Gentiles with the priestly duty of proclaiming the gospel of God, so that the Gentiles might become an offering acceptable to God, sanctified by the Holy Spirit.

Therefore I glory in Christ Jesus in my service to God. I will not venture to speak of anything except what Christ has accomplished through me in leading the Gentiles to obey God by what I have said and done—by the power of signs and miracles, through the power of the Spirit. So from Jerusalem all the way around to Illyricum, I have fully proclaimed the gospel of Christ. It has always been my ambition to preach the gospel where Christ was not known, so that I would not be building on someone else's foundation. Rather, as it is written:

> "Those who were not told about him will see,
>   and those who have not heard will
>   understand."

This is why I have often been hindered from coming to you.

But now that there is no more place for me to work in these regions, and since I have been longing for many years to see you, I plan to do so when I go to Spain. I hope to visit you while passing through and to have you assist me on my journey there, after I have enjoyed your company for a while. Now, however, I am on my way to Jerusalem in the service of the saints there. For Macedonia and Achaia were pleased to make a contribution for the poor among the saints in Jerusalem. They were pleased to do it, and indeed they owe it to them. For if the Gentiles have shared in the Jews' spiritual blessings, they owe it to the Jews to share with them their material blessings. So after I have completed this task and have made sure that they have received this fruit, I will go to Spain and visit you on the way. I know that when I come to you, I will come in the full measure of the blessing of Christ.

I urge you, brothers, by our Lord Jesus Christ and by the love of the Spirit, to join me in my struggle by praying to God for me. Pray that I may be rescued from the unbelievers in Judea and that my service in Jerusalem may be acceptable to the saints there, so that by God's will I may come to you with joy and together with you be refreshed. The God of peace be with you all. Amen.

Paul's Glory

*Therefore I glory in Christ Jesus in my service to
God. I will not venture to speak of anything except what Christ has accomplished through
me in leading the Gentiles to obey God.*

ROMANS 15:17–18

The miracles that need to be done today are not healing the
sick or raising the dead but bringing dead souls to life to
believe on Jesus Christ as Lord and Savior and then to be
changed by him.

Someone once asked a preacher whether he could turn
water into wine as Jesus did. He answered that he could
do something better than that. He told about an alcoholic
who had neglected his family but who had been brought to
Christ by hearing the gospel. The preacher said, "We didn't
turn water into wine, but we turned whisky into milk for
his babies."

So it has always been. As Christ's people have taken the
gospel to the farthest reaches of the world, pagans living in
darkest spiritual night have been brought to gospel day, the
despairing have been given a sure and lasting hope, liars have
been turned into men and women of truth, people of loose
morals have become righteous and upright, and those who

have been lazy with no real goals in life have been captured for Jesus and have lived industrious lives for his glory. Such acts have fulfilled Jesus's words when he said, "Anyone who has faith in me will do what I have been doing. He will do even greater things than these, because I am going to the Father" (John 14:12).

If even the angels in heaven rejoice whenever a sinner comes to Christ (Luke 15:10), should it not be our goal and glory to work faithfully and industriously to see it happen too?

But remember, although the conversion of the lost is our glory to the extent that we participate by carrying the gospel to them, it is ours only because it is Jesus Christ's first of all, because he is at work within us. Paul said, "I glory *in Christ Jesus*" (Rom. 15:17).

What do you glory in? Are you filled with zeal for the conversion of the lost? Pray now for individuals you know, that they will experience the miracle of rebirth to the glory of the Lord Jesus Christ.

Part 22: Final Greetings

Romans 16:1–27

I commend to you our sister Phoebe, a servant of the church in Cenchrea. I ask you to receive her in the Lord in a way worthy of the saints and to give her any help she may need from you, for she has been a great help to many people, including me.

Greet Priscilla and Aquila, my fellow workers in Christ Jesus. They risked their lives for me. Not only I but all the churches of the Gentiles are grateful to them.

Greet also the church that meets at their house.

Greet my dear friend Epenetus, who was the first convert to Christ in the province of Asia.

Greet Mary, who worked very hard for you.

Greet Andronicus and Junias, my relatives who have been in prison with me. They are outstanding among the apostles, and they were in Christ before I was.

Greet Ampliatus, whom I love in the Lord.

Greet Urbanus, our fellow worker in Christ, and my dear friend Stachys.

Greet Apelles, tested and approved in Christ.

Greet those who belong to the household of Aristobulus.

Greet Herodion, my relative.

Greet those in the household of Narcissus who are in the Lord.

Greet Tryphena and Tryphosa, those women who work hard in the Lord.

Greet my dear friend Persis, another woman who has worked very hard in the Lord.

Greet Rufus, chosen in the Lord, and his mother, who has been a mother to me, too.

Greet Asyncritus, Phlegon, Hermes, Patrobas, Hermas and the brothers with them.

Greet Philologus, Julia, Nereus and his sister, and Olympas and all the saints with them.

Greet one another with a holy kiss.

All the churches of Christ send greetings.

I urge you, brothers, to watch out for those who cause divisions and put obstacles in your way that are contrary to the teaching you have learned. Keep away from them. For such people are not serving our Lord Christ, but their own appetites. By smooth talk and flattery they deceive the minds of naive people. Everyone has heard about your obedience, so I am full of joy over you; but I want you to be wise about what is good, and innocent about what is evil.

The God of peace will soon crush Satan under your feet.

The grace of our Lord Jesus be with you.

The Third Benediction

The grace of our Lord Jesus be with you.
ROMANS 16:20

Paul's benediction is a prayer. That is, it is a request that the grace of the Lord Jesus Christ would continue to be with his readers and that they might experience even more of it than they had before. What can this mean? If God has been so abundantly gracious to us, how can we continue to grow in grace? There are at least four ways Paul's prayer can and should be taken.

1. *We need to be settled in the great grace doctrines.* There are several ways we can fail to be settled in grace. We can allow something other than Jesus Christ to be at the center of our lives. We can forget how gracious God has been and therefore become harsh or cruel with others. We can substitute the mere form of Christianity for the gospel. The cure for these ills is to be so aware of the nature of the grace of God in saving us that we become enamored of Jesus Christ and never forget that it is by grace alone that we have been brought out of death and darkness into God's marvelous life and light.

2. *We need to grow in the knowledge of God's grace.* Knowledge of the grace of God is not a static thing. There-

fore, we need to seek continually to grow in that knowledge. Peter wrote, "Grow in grace and knowledge of our Lord and Savior Jesus Christ" (2 Peter 3:18). To do so we must study the Word of God and meditate on its teachings.

3. *We need to exercise the gift for serving others that God has given each of us.* We do not often think of the grace of God and the gifts of God as belonging together, but a number of passages combine the two ideas. Peter wrote that each Christian "should use whatever gift he has received to serve others, faithfully administering God's grace in its various forms" (1 Peter 4:10). Paul wrote to the church at Ephesus, "To each one of us grace has been given as Christ apportioned it" (Eph. 4:7). Therefore, when we pray for the grace of the Lord Jesus Christ to be with God's people, one thing we might mean is that each Christian should use the gift he or she has been given by God to help others.

4. *We need a continuing supply of grace in order to complete the work God assigns us.* Paul was conscious of having received grace to carry out his calling as an apostle. But he also knew that he needed it constantly, and he was aware that others needed a continual supply of grace to do the work God had assigned to them. Obviously you and I do also.

Pray for God's grace to be upon you today, that you may be settled in the great doctrines of grace, that you may grow in knowledge of God's grace, and that through his grace you may serve others.

Timothy, my fellow worker, sends his greetings to you, as do Lucius, Jason and Sosipater, my relatives.

I, Tertius, who wrote down this letter, greet you in the Lord.

Gaius, whose hospitality I and the whole church here enjoy, sends you his greetings.

Erastus, who is the city's director of public works, and our brother Quartus send you their greetings.

Now to him who is able to establish you by my gospel and the proclamation of Jesus Christ, according to the revelation of the mystery hidden for long ages past, but now revealed and made known through the prophetic writings by the command of the eternal God, so that all nations might believe and obey him—to the only wise God be glory forever through Jesus Christ! Amen.

Glory to the Only Wise God

To the only wise God be glory for-
ever through Jesus Christ! Amen.

ROMANS 16:27

It is appropriate that we think carefully about this last word
of the letter. What does it mean to say "Amen"?

Amen is a wonderfully rich word. It is found in nearly
half the languages of the world, and it refers to what is true,
firm, or faithful. In its intransitive form it means to be shored
up—to be firm, unshaken. It means to be faithful, trustworthy,
sure, something that one can lean on or build upon. In this
sense it is used as a name for God in Isaiah 65:16, though the
New International Version translates it as the word *truth*. The
verse says, "Whoever invokes a blessing in the land will do
so by the God of truth." But the Hebrew text actually says
"by the God of the Amen." It is a way of saying that God is
a sure and solid foundation for those who lean on him. He
is utterly reliable.

We use this word at the end of something God says. When
God says something he begins with "Amen, amen": "What I
am about to say is true; pay attention." For our part, we hear
the words, repeat them, and then say "Amen," meaning that

we agree with God's declaration. We set our seal to our belief that the Word of God is true and that he is faithful.

That is what Paul is doing as he comes to the end of Romans and offers these last words of doxology. He is setting his seal to God's truth, saying that he believes God's Word. Can you do that? Can you add your "Amen" to what Paul has written?

For my part, that is what I am determined to do. There is much in this world I do not understand. There is much even about the ways of God I do not understand. But what I do understand I believe, and to God's declaration of these eternal truths I say a hearty, "Amen!" "There is no one righteous, not even one" (Rom. 3:10). Amen! "For all have sinned and fall short of the glory of God" (Rom. 3:23). Amen! "For the wages of sin is death, but the gift of God is eternal life in Christ Jesus our Lord" (Rom. 6:23). Amen! "Neither death nor life, neither angels nor demons, neither the present nor the future, nor any powers, neither height nor depth, nor anything else in all creation, will be able to separate us from the love of God that is in Christ Jesus our Lord" (Rom. 8:38–39). Amen!

"Then all the people said, 'Amen'" (1 Chron. 16:36).

It is right to say "Amen" to all that has been taught in these devotions on Romans. But what particular truth has impacted you, whether to comfort you or convict you? Hold that truth before the Lord in prayer and conclude with "Amen!"

Notes

Preface

1. James Montgomery Boice, *Romans: Justification by Faith*, vol. 1 (Grand Rapids: Baker, 1991), 10.

2. James Montgomery Boice, *Romans: The New Humanity*, vol. 4 (Grand Rapids: Baker, 1995), xii.

Introduction

1. Saint Augustine, *Confessions*, trans. J. G. Pilkington, in *Basic Writings of Saint Augustine*, ed. Whitney J. Oates (New York: Random House, 1948), vol. 1, 126.

2. J. H. Merle D'Aubigné, *The Life and Times of Martin Luther*, trans. H. White (Chicago: Moody Press, 1958), 55–56.

3. Martin Luther, *Commentary on the Epistle to the Romans*, trans. J. Theodore Mueller (Grand Rapids: Zondervan, 1954), xi.

4. F. Godet, *Commentary on St. Paul's Epistle to the Romans*, trans. A. Cusin (Edinburgh: T. &. T. Clark, n.d.), vol. 1, 1.

5. D. M. Lloyd-Jones, *Romans: An Exposition of Chapter 1, The Gospel of God* (Grand Rapids: Zondervan, 1985), 25

6. Ibid.

7. Robert Haldane, *An Exposition of the Epistle to the Romans* (MacDill AFB: MacDonald Publishing, 1958), 14.

Day 13

1. Quoted without giving the name of the writer by Donald Grey Barnhouse, *God's Freedom: Exposition of Bible Doctrines, Taking the Epistle to the Romans as a Point of Departure, vol. 6*, Romans 6:1–7:25 (Grand Rapids: Wm. B. Eerdmans, 1961), 13.

2. Ibid.

Day 19

1. C. S. Lewis, "The Weight of Glory" in *The Weight of Glory and Other Addresses* (New York: Macmillan/Collier, 1980), 7.

Day 20

1. Haldane, *Romans,* 407–8.

2. This story is told by Ray C. Stedman, *From Guilt to Glory*, vol. 1, *Hope for the Helpless* (Portland: Multnomah, 1978), 302.

Day 31

1. Donald Grey Barnhouse, *One Body in Christ*, booklet 68 in the series of expositions on Romans (Philadelphia: The Bible Study Hour, 1956), 11.

Day 32

1. Leon Morris, *The Epistle to the Romans* (Grand Rapids: Eerdmans, 1988), 451.

Day 35

1. John Murray, *The Epistle to the Romans*, 2 vols. in 1 (Grand Rapids: Eerdmans, 1968), vol. 2, 175.

Hymns by James Montgomery Boice

Dr. Boice's final writings were not sermons but hymns. Encouraged by Tenth's music director, Dr. Paul S. Jones, he began writing hymns in the summer of 1999 and continued writing up to his last days the following spring. An expository preacher, his hymns likewise were expositions of Scripture texts. Not surprisingly, of the first five hymns, four were based on texts from Romans. They are presented here in the order in which they were written.

Fittingly, the first hymn, "Give Praise to God," is based on Romans 11:33–36, the passage regarded as the theme of Dr. Boice's life, and is inscribed on the commemorative plaque in Tenth Presbyterian Church's sanctuary. "How Marvelous, How Wise, How Great" and "Hallelujah!" present the closing verses of chapter eight, the chapter Dr. Boice regarded as the greatest in the Bible. "Heaven's Gift" lays forth the gospel presentation of Romans 3:21–28.

Dr. Boice loved hymns, as can be seen in his commentaries and sermons, which include many hymn quotes and even expositions of hymns. He loved to sing hymns, as I can attest standing beside him in the pulpit as he sang with strong voice, rocking on his heels, often with the hymnal closed and his hands in his back pockets. As important as he regarded preaching to be, he believed that theology got into the hearts of people through music.

These four hymn selections are taken from the hymnbook *Hymns for a Modern Reformation.* I am thankful to Dr. Jones, who composed the music, for granting permission to print them in this devotional. The hymnbook containing fourteen of Dr. Boice's hymns is distributed by the Alliance of Confessing Evangelicals, 1716 Spruce Street, Philadelphia, PA 19103.

Give Praise to God

" "Give Praise to God" was the first of the new Reformation hymns to be written. The occasion was the fiftieth anniversary celebration of The Bible Study Hour on September 12, 1999. The weekend's theme was *Toward a New Reformation*, and the text for the Sunday morning sermon was Romans 11:36, the last verse of the magnificent doxology that closes the great doctrinal chapters of that book. Verse 36 is the climax and the Apostle's testimony to all he has written. So the verse offered itself, particularly the last line "To Him be the glory forever! Amen" as an obvious refrain for the hymn. The stanzas of the hymn follow the preceding sections of the doxology, the first expressing the thoughts of verse 33, asking the worshiper to praise God for his infinite knowledge and wisdom, and acknowledging that God's ways are beyond our understanding.

The second recognizes, as does verse 34 of Romans 11, that because God's knowledge and wisdom are beyond our comprehension, no one can counsel God. Rather he is our true Counselor to whom we should look for wisdom and guidance. The third stanza points out that we cannot give anything to God either, as if the Creator of all things could need anything. The fourth and final stanza expresses the first part of verse 36, acknowledging, as we must, that all things come both from and through God himself and lead rightly to the worship of God by his redeemed creation.

The majestic sweep of the doxology "For from him and through him and to him are all things; to him be the glory forever. Amen" displays a powerful rhythm and rhetoric well-suited to musical expression. The hymn's four stanzas of eight-syllable lines provide a regular and stately framework for this noble text. To complement this regularity while avoiding the possibility of the music sounding too "fixed" or square, the setting is in three-quarter time, grouped in four-measure phrases with half-note stresses falling on significant syllables. The key of D major, often associated with celebration and "royal" music, particularly in the Baroque because of its accessibility for trumpets and timpani, was chosen for these associative reasons as well as for its natural brilliance. The melody has a British flavor and finds its climax at the text "heaven's high throne" where the rhythm, constant in the other five lines, is intentionally altered so as to point heavenward. The tune name {*Soli Deo*} ("God alone") is an abbreviated form of the Reformation's *soli Deo gloria* ("Glory to God alone").

FIRST SUNG: SEPTEMBER 12, 1999

Give Praise to God

1

For from him and through him and to him are all things.
To him be the glory forever! Amen. Rom. 11:36

1. Give praise to God who reigns a - bove for per - fect
2. No one can coun - sel God all - wise or truths un -
3. Noth - ing ex - ists that God might need for all things
4. Cre - a - tion, life, sal - va - tion too, and all things

know - ledge, wis - dom, love; his judg - ments are di -
veil to his sharp eyes; he marks our paths be -
good from him pro - ceed. We praise him as our
else both good and true, come from and through our

vine, de - vout, his paths be - yond all tra - cing out.
hind, be - fore; he is our stead - fast Coun - se - lor.
Lord, and yet we nev - er place God in our debt.
God al - ways, and fill our hearts with grate - ful praise.

Come, lift your voice to heaven's high throne,

And glo - ry give to God a - lone!

Based on Romans 11:33-36
James Montgomery Boice, 1999

SOLI DEO
L.M.ref.
Paul S. Jones, 1999

How Marvelous, How Wise, How Great

There are few passages in the entire Bible that trace the full scope of God's purpose with those he has determined to save as does Romans 8:28-31. The passage begins with God's election of a people for himself, speaks of his determination to conform them to the likeness of Jesus Christ, and then completes what some have called the great "golden chain" that ends with calling, justification and glorification. The unbrokenness of the chain is important, because each act leads to the next, and in each God is describing something he has done, even the glorification of his elect in spite of the fact that it has not yet taken place for all in time.

This is the reason for the interlocking rhyme scheme that pervades and links the four stanzas. The stanzas follow the biblical text and introduce Calvinistic doctrine. The first stanza begins by marveling at God's purpose to regenerate a faithless, fallen man. The second reflects on the election of that individual and notes that God's predestining purpose is to conform him to the likeness of Jesus Christ. After rejoicing in our justification and glorification in stanza three, as Romans 8 does in verse 30, the hymn concludes in stanza four by saying that nothing remains for us now but to embrace God and his grace, run our race well, and praise God forever.

The interlocking rhyme scheme of the scripture-rich poetry in these four stanzas is matched with an appropriately balanced tune. Each six-line stanza is formally constructed as AAB-AAB where the "B" rhyme becomes "A" for the following stanza (For example, "plan" and "man" of stanza one lead to "began", "plan", "man" and "can" in stanza two; B becomes A). The musical setting retains the same dotted rhythm in all four "A" phrases and maintains straight quarter notes in the two "B" phrases. The peak of the melody and harmony occurs at the end of the first AAB grouping, which, in each verse, is an important textual point of arrival. The two "A" phrases make statements that the "B" phrase summarizes or to which it responds. The use of a naturalized D within key signature of four flats "opens up" the "B" phrase in the fifth full measure cadence and is balanced with another in measure 10. The tune name {*Spruce Street*} marks the location of its composition as well as the site of Tenth Presbyterian Church.

FIRST SUNG: OCTOBER 17, 199─

Aside:
As an example of Dr. Boice's biblical scholarship and critical thinking about his hymns, here is some commentary written to the composer about revisions made to this text:

> In the second stanza I want to change "astonishing decree" to "a glorious decree." "Glory" is a biblical word; "astonishing" is not. Plus it should sing better. In the third stanza I am changing "that glorified I soon may be" to "and glorified I soon will be." This makes it certain, which "may" does not necessarily convey.

How Marvelous, How Wise, How Great

2

For those God foreknew he also predestined... called... justified... glorified.
Rom. 8:29-30

1. How mar - ve- lous, how wise, how great, how
2. Fore - known be - fore the world be - gan, ac -
3. He bore my sin on Cal - vary's tree and
4. What have I now but to em - brace the

in - fi - nite to con - tem - plate: Je - ho - vah's sav - ing
cord- ing to his gra - cious plan, God des - tined I must
right-eous - ness be - stowed on me that I might see his
God who saved me from dis - grace and love him ev - er -

plan. He saw me in my lost es - tate yet
be con - formed to Je - sus Christ, the man, who
face. God jus - ti - fied me, set me free, and
more; and with con - tent - ment run my race my

pur - posed to re - gen - er - ate this faith - less, fal - len man.
lived and loved as no man can: a glo - ri - ous de - cree.
glo - ri - fied I soon will be: how mar - ve - lous this grace.
eyes fixed ev - er on his face to praise him and a - dore.

Based on Romans 8:28-31
James Montgomery Boice, 1999

©1999 TenthMusic. All rights reserved.

SPRUCE STREET
8.8.6.8.8.6.
Paul S. Jones, 1999

Heaven's Gift

There is probably no passage in the New Testament that contains the gospel in more condensed form than Roman 3:21-26. Following upon Paul's devastating description of sin (extent, nature and consequences) which ends, "Therefore no one will be declared righteous in his sight by observing the law; rather, through the law we become conscious of sin" (verse 20), Paul introduces the mighty phrase "But God," followed by some of the most powerful words in the Christian's vocabulary: righteousness, propitiation, justification, redemption, and faith. Each of these words, in turn, becomes a theme of the subsequent stanzas. Also, the final phrase of each stanza gives us its climax: A righteousness from God made known; And turned God's wrath from me aside; Be just and justifier too; For all is Christ and Christ my all; And rest in God's amazing grace (an intentional quote).

"The source of our justification is the grace of God (v. 24) and the ground of our justification is the work of Christ (v. 25). The channel of our justification is faith (v. 25 ff.). There are eight occurrences of the word 'faith' in verses 21-31...and faith involves three things:

1. Faith involves content.
2. Faith involves an assent to the Bible's teaching.
3. Faith involves commitment.

Justification is by the grace of God *through faith*. You must commit yourself to Jesus." [1]

The hymn tune {*Sola Fide*} was written in August, 1999, in the composer's hometown of Rothesay, New Brunswick (Canada) while on a brief summer vacation. In fact, it was first named "Rothesay." One of the goals of author and composer was to include a hymn for each "sola" of the Reformation. It became apparent after much thought and prayer that "Heaven's Gift" was indeed our "Faith Alone" hymn, and so the tune was renamed. This setting in 3/2 time employs a metrical change in the third line to better emphasize the text which is written in long meter (L.M.) or 8.8.8.8. It serves to rhythmically propel the final line which contains the goal, result, or climactic phrase of each stanza. The melody employs all eight notes of the diatonic major scale, but it has a pentatonic feel to it especially in the second system where only five different notes are used. Harmonically reminiscent of other Welsh hymn tunes, the joy and celebration of the text are echoed in the direct, functional harmony and the rolling ascent and descent of the melody, which spans an octave and a fourth in B-flat major.

FIRST SUNG: REFORMATION SUNDAY, OCTOBER 31, 1999

[1] James Montgomery Boice. *The Glory of God's Grace*, Grand Rapids: Kregel Pub., 1999, pp.83-88.

Heaven's Gift

3

*This righteousness from God comes through faith in Jesus Christ
to all who believe. Rom. 3:22*

1. When far from God and lost in sin I____ took God's book and looked with-in, I found a gift from heav-en's throne, a right-eous-ness from God made known.
2. That gift Christ won at dread-ful cost: pro - pi - ti - a - tion for the lost. My sub - sti - tute, con - demned he died, and turned God's wrath from me a - side.
3. Now in Christ's right - eous - ness a - lone I____ stand be - fore God's awe - some throne, and grasp what on - ly God could do: be just and jus - ti - fi - er too.
4. Christ paid the price to set me free: his____ blood poured out on Cal - vary's tree. Now noth - ing as my own I'll call, for all is Christ's and Christ my all.
5. All mer - it, boast - ing set a - side, by____ faith a - lone I'm jus - ti - fied. Be - fore the throne I take my place and rest in God's a - maz - ing grace.

Based on Romans 3:21-28
James Montgomery Boice, 1999

SOLA FIDE
L.M.
Paul S. Jones, 1999

Hallelujah!

The love of God is eternal. Its origins can be found in eternity past and its end is to be found in eternity future. To state it another way, it has no end at all. Paul mentions two classes of possible "separators" in the list of 17 potential threats to a Christian's relationship to God's love: 1) natural enemies, and 2) supernatural enemies, and he denies the effectiveness of either.[2]

> As Paul gets to the end of his statement of the everlasting and victorious character of God's love, he reaches the high point of this epistle. He speaks of 'the love of God [which is] *in Christ Jesus.*'...There is no other way to know the love of God personally; therefore there is really no other way to know the love of God at all. It must begin by our commitment to Christ. God has decreed that it is only in Christ that his great, infinite, giving, sovereign and eternal love for sinners may be known.[3]

The answer to every question raised by Paul regarding the ability of these natural and supernatural powers to separate us from the love of God is the same–"nothing." The truth of this security and assurance should cause all Christians everywhere to respond by singing, "Hallelujah!" It is only because of the saving work of Christ and the preserving work of the Holy Spirit that we can thus answer and thus respond.

Since this hymn boldly affirms the doctrine of the perseverance of the saints, the tune is aptly named {*Perseverance*}. An unusual meter (7.7.7.6), the numerous interrogative phrases and the assertive final line presented an interesting compositional challenge both rhetorically and musically. There is a certainty, an almost fist-pounding emphasis in "Nothing. Hallelujah!" that requires corporate solidarity and energy in execution. The rhythmic setting of those two words was crucial to achieving this goal. The melodic shape here follows the cadence of the speaking voice with one purposeful exception–the final syllable "jah" ends higher, stronger and longer than "lu." But why shouldn't it? If we understand that "Hallelujah" means "Praise the LORD" ("jah" standing for "Yahweh"), it makes sense. God is the object of our praise, as is always the case in true worship. The melody of the first three phrases follows a sequential pattern (measures 2, 4, and 6 employ a melodic structure in stepwise descent, higher with each phrase). This pattern emulates the three phrases and questions that build on each other until the arrival of the powerful answer which is followed by the thankful response of God's people to this truth. The key, D-flat major, was selected for its warmth, power and resonance as well as for the five flats, since the doctrine of perseverance is the fifth point of Calvinism.

FIRST SUNG: JANUARY 21, 200

---

[2] James Montgomery Boice. *Foundations of the Christian Faith.* rev. ed., Downers Grove, IL: InterVarsity Press, 1986, p.338.

[3] Ibid., pp.338-339.

Hallelujah!

5

*[Nothing]... will be able to separate us from the love of God
that is in Christ Jesus our Lord. Rom. 8:39*

1. What can sep - a - rate my soul
2. Trou - ble, hard - ship, dan - ger, sword
3. An - gels, de - mons, now or then?
4. Vic - tors we're or - dained to be
5. We face death for God each day;

from the God who made me whole, wrote my name in
brought by those who hate my Lord? Slan - der here? Or
Wick - ed - ness dreamed up by men? Per - se - cu - tions
by the God who set us free; what can there - fore
what can pluck us from his way? Let God's peo - ple

hea - ven's scroll?____ Noth - ing. Hal - le - lu - jah!
no re - ward?____ Noth - ing. Hal - le - lu - jah!
come a - gain?____ Noth - ing. Hal - le - lu - jah!
con - quer me?____ Noth - ing. Hal - le - lu - jah!
ev - er say,____ "Noth - ing." Hal - le - lu - jah!

Based on Romans 8:35-39
James Montgomery Boice, 1999

PERSEVERANCE
7.7.7.6.
Paul S. Jones, 1999

Classic Commentary Series by Boice

All twenty-seven volumes of the popular Boice Expositional
Commentary series are now available on one convenient and
portable CD-ROM. Boice's clear language and approachable style
make these commentaries accessible and enlightening for a wide
range of students of the Bible.

The books included are:

- Genesis (3 vols.)
- Joshua
- Psalms (3 vols.)
- Daniel
- Nehemiah
- The Minor Prophets (2 vols.)
- Matthew (2 vols.)

- The Sermon on the Mount
- John (5 vols.)
- Acts
- Romans (4 vols.)
- Ephesians
- Philippians
- The Epistles of John

James Montgomery Boice (1938–2000) was senior
pastor of Tenth Presbyterian Church in Philadelphia, Pennsylvania.
He was also president and cofounder of the Alliance of Confessing
Evangelicals, the parent organization of The Bible Study Hour, on
which he was a speaker for more than thirty years.

Individual commentaries may also be
purchased.

To learn more about the series, visit:
www.bakerbooks.com/Boice

BakerBooks
a division of Baker Publishing Group
www.BakerBooks.com